Disciples

Year 2

G000147500

prayer

Jonathan Brownson

Grand Rapids, Michigan

This study is part of *Disciples,* year 2, a comprehensive multiyear faith formation program for adults. Year 2 studies build on the foundation laid by the studies in year 1.

Year 2 includes the following five-session study guides, which feature five daily readings for each session:

- Prayer
- Reading the Bible
- Worship
- Living in Community
- Overcoming Sin

Unless otherwise indicated, Scripture quotations in this publication are from the Holy Bible, Today's New International Version, © 2001, 2005 by the International Bible Society. All rights reserved worldwide. Used by permission.

Disciples: Prayer, © 2008 by Faith Alive Christian Resources, 2850 Kalamazoo Ave. SE, Grand Rapids, MI 49560. All rights reserved. With the exception of brief excerpts for review purposes, no part of this book may be reproduced in any manner whatsoever without written permission from the publisher. Printed in the United States of America.

We welcome your comments. Call us at 1-800-333-8300 or e-mail us at editors@faithaliveresources.org.

Contents

Introduction

Most of you who pick up this book are already following Jesus. Your trail guide along the way has been Disciples year 1 from Faith Alive Christian Resources.

What have you seen? What areas would you like to explore more? Where might Jesus be inviting you further into his purposes for your life?

I'm guessing—or better yet, hypothesizing—that one of the things you have noticed along the way is the importance of prayer in Jesus' life.

I am hypothesizing not because I have "incomplete information" (the Scriptures tell us more than enough about Jesus at prayer). My problem is "incomplete application." When it comes to prayer, I as writer—and perhaps you as reader—feel educated beyond actual practice. We know more about the importance of prayer than we do about praying. Having this book in hand doesn't mean we have prayer in habit. We have a common interest, but not common competence.

> **Word Alert**
>
> **A *hypothesis* is a proposal intended to explain certain facts or observations based on incomplete information.**

We are perhaps at the same stage of following Jesus as his first followers were in Luke 11:1-4. Notice something with me about this passage. It's the only recorded time in the entire New Testament that Jesus' followers actually *ask* him to teach them. In Luke 11 we look through the window of Scripture into the needs of Jesus' first followers.

Of all the things these disciples feel they need from the master, they need help with prayer most of all. They need help—and Jesus is ready to provide it. He gives them what we usually call the Lord's Prayer (but we could also refer to it as the Disciples' Prayer).

Jesus' first followers know they don't have a prayer, so he gives them one. What about you? Do you want the master's help too?

In Other Words

Why do Christians need to pray?

Because prayer is the most important part of the thankfulness God requires of us. And also because God gives his grace and Holy Spirit only to those who pray continually and groan inwardly, asking God for these gifts and thanking him for them.

—Heidelberg Catechism, Q&A 116

Our youngest son starts college this year. He has me thinking about my start at the University of Michigan (don't ask when). I waited in long lines and paid big bucks (not nearly as big as today, of course) to ask an institution the same question the disciples ask Jesus: "Will you teach me?" The institution offered a few options as the following (partial!) list of available Liberal Arts and Sciences courses suggests:

> Afroamerican & African Studies; Arabic, Armenian, Persian, Turkish, and Islamic Studies; Ancient Civilization & Biblical Studies; Aerospace Science; American Culture; Anthropology; Archaeology . . . and that's just the "A"s!

There's a lot to learn, isn't there, on a variety of subjects!

So it's striking that the only class Jesus' disciples sign up for and ask him to teach is a course on prayer. Incidentally, that class isn't mentioned on the U of M list. It wasn't on my seminary course list either.

For the very first students in Jesus' very first class, the first topic was prayer. Of all the things Jesus could have taught them, they wanted him to teach them to pray.

Word Alert

There are many definitions of the word *prayer.* Muslims, for instance, pray five times a day as an act of honoring Allah. The specific word that Jesus and his disciples use in Luke 11:1 is *Proseuxomai,* which means to ask for something. While we certainly praise God in prayer, at its heart prayer is asking, seeking, knocking at heaven's door (Matt. 7:7). *What* we ask for, *how* we ask, and *why* are the objects of our exploration together.

Is that the way you feel? I do. I want to have a relationship with the Lord Jesus, and through him with the one he called Abba. I so much want and need to know how to pray. If you feel the same way, let's do these guides and devotionals together. Let's sign up with the first followers for the course of a lifetime.

About This Book

If you have been using *Disciples,* year 1, you will notice a difference in year 2. As you learn more about what it means to follow Jesus, we are asking you to commit to growing as disciples.

So in this book, and in the others that follow, each small group discussion is preceded by a series of five daily readings or devotionals. We invite you to take the time to read these before the small group discussion—both to deepen your walk as disciples and to be better prepared for a fruitful discussion together.

You may use the daily readings for your own personal devotions or you may read them with others (your family, a prayer group, roommates). At the end of each daily reading there is a set of questions to ponder or discuss, depending on how you are using them. Reading them day by day, thinking about them throughout the week, and sharing them with others will deepen your understanding and help bring the practice of prayer from your mind to your heart.

You will also notice that Scripture references are scattered throughout the daily readings. Please take the time to look them up, ponder them, and perhaps read the verses around them. That will help make your devotional time much more fruitful and deepen your understanding and practice of prayer.

Session 1
The Lord's Prayer

Abba 1

"When you pray, say 'Father [Abba] . . .'"

—Luke 11:2

Followers of Jesus focus on prayer. Out of all the things that could be learned, all the courses that could be taken on prayer, Jesus' disciples begin with Prayer 101.

Jesus could have said to them (and to us), "This course is restricted to advanced students and you don't qualify." He could have said, "We have cancelled that section due to lack of interest—it took you too long to figure out that this is important." Jesus was, after all, the master at prayer.

What's interesting is that the disciples were certainly not ignorant about prayer. The Jews were and are a praying people. Their Bible included a whole book dedicated to prayer—the Psalms. They had learned many prayers in the synagogues. But they wanted to learn to pray as Jesus prayed, which was different from anything they had ever heard before.

The key to Jesus' life of prayer is the simple Aramaic word with which his prayer begins: *Abba.*

Word Alert

***Aramaic* is not a men's cologne but the everyday language Jesus spoke as he conversed with those around him. While closely related to Hebrew, it had a distinct flavor, something like the "Spanglish" used by some Hispanic people in North America.**

Jesus' prayer, of course, is not about coming up with the *right* words; it's about *first* words, childish words. It's more relational than rational. God is more interested in establishing a heart-to-heart relationship with people than in the proper protocol for addressing the deity. So Jesus makes it as simple and natural as possible to get started.

Jesus addresses God as *Abba*, Father. This form of address is not about maleness; rather, it's about the relationship. He's introducing his disciples into the relationship he has as the Son of the one he calls *Abba*. In this simplest language of a child, Jesus is inviting them and us into the family. While Jesus is God's "only Son" (in the words of the Apostles' Creed), Jesus' followers become God's sons and daughters through him.

Word Alert

***Abba* was Jesus' own unique way of addressing God. Though it's translated "Father," it's closer to the word children might use to address their own dad. It has the flavor of deep intimacy. And it was evidently so special that Paul, writing to Greek-speaking Gentiles, preserves it in the original Aramaic rather than translate it. "The Spirit you received does not make you slaves, so that you live in fear again; rather, the Spirit you received brought about your adoption to sonship. And by him we cry, "*Abba*, Father" (Rom. 8:15; see also Gal. 4:6).**

Do you remember the first word you heard from your own child or from a beloved niece or nephew? Did it warm your heart to hear such a sound? Was your first tendency to resist? Of course not! As Jesus said, "Which of you, if your son asks for bread, will give him a stone?" (Matt. 7:9).

For the gospel writer, *Abba* feels just like that. It has the same power and passion. It brings us with astonishing intimacy into the Lord's practice of prayer.

Jesus has been speaking the language of prayer with his disciples like a parent in front of children. For the first ten chapters of Luke, they have seen and heard him talk to God as *Abba*. Now Jesus invites them to give it a try.

In teaching them to pray, Jesus wants his disciples to learn a new language of love—the love that existed between the Father and the Son from eternity. And now we can become part of that love, that divine "family."

Think It Over

1. What is the first word you normally use when you pray? Why?
2. Sometimes words are hard for our lips to say. Sometimes they are hard for our hearts to feel. Do you personally use the word *Abba* to address God? What picture of prayer does it bring to mind?
3. How does that picture impact your prayer?

In Other Words

"This address is employed at the invitation of Jesus, the elder brother, as a sign of membership in Jesus' spiritual family. Through Jesus the believer comes into the presence of the one whom Jesus called "Abba, Father." . . . To use this address is to enter into the relationship that Jesus enjoyed with God."

—Stanley J. Grenz, *The Cry for the Kingdom*

Live It Out

As you pray today, address God as *Abba.* Notice how it feels to you. Perhaps throughout the day you might just whisper or think *Abba* as a sort of one-word prayer. See how it links whatever you are doing or thinking with the One with whom Jesus has brought you into such a close, loving, and intimate relationship.

Our Father 2

"This, then, is how you should pray: 'Our Father. . . .'"

—Matthew 6:9

Prayer is person-al. When someone says "it's personal," sometimes what they mean is that it is private. They don't want to share it. The interviewer for *Entertainment Tonight* asks a movie star whether she colors her hair. Never mind, is the reply. It's personal.

Is that the way you feel about prayer? Do you feel it's best done in the privacy of your own home?

That seems to be what Jesus suggests: "But when you pray, go into your room, close the door and pray to your Father, who is unseen . . ." (Matt. 6:6). Don't be public about your piety. What you pray and how often you pray is *your* business; it's private like the real color of your hair.

But is that what Jesus is really talking about? I don't think so. Because after he tells the disciples to go to their room, he tells them to say *our* Father.

In fact, the whole prayer uses the plural possessive pronoun—*our* daily bread, *our* debts, *our* temptations, *our* struggle with the evil one. Why is that? It's not an attempt to stake a claim to the Father and his gifts: "ours" as opposed to "theirs." Rather it's a constant reminder that when we call God our *Abba*, we can never stand before God all alone. We cannot have a private relationship with God.

I cannot talk to my *Abba* without including all my brothers and sisters. Knowing God as *Abba* means that I am instantly and deeply related to all his other human creatures, perhaps even his non-human creatures. I cannot pray for myself without at the same time praying for them.

In my prayer closet I am joined by Saudi multimillionaires and Haitian peasants. I pray with and for my dearest friends and my bitterest enemies. I pray with and for people from every nation, tribe, and language. I pray with and for Christians, Muslims, Buddhists, and atheists. I am joined in prayer by gang members, pimps, prostitutes, all the homeless who seek refuge at the local shelter, starving babies, people dying of AIDS, old men and women with Alzheimer's, and death row inmates. The One who is our Father loves all his children, whether they know it or not.

We cannot separate the vertical and the horizontal. We cannot talk to God while we are ignoring his myriad other children. When we are talking to the Father "from whom every family in heaven and earth derives its name" (Eph. 3:15), we cannot have just a private conversation.

"Our Father," demands of us in our most intimate moment of prayer to believe and acknowledge God's desire to include everyone in his family. If we ever forget that, we lose the capacity to really pray.

The first word in prayer is about our relationship with God. We love the Lord our God with all our heart soul, mind and strength when we say *Abba*. The second word in prayer (and the second command) is about relationships with others. We love our neighbor as ourselves, which is why we pray, *"Our Abba."*

How much are you thinking of others when you pray? Maybe it is time we spent an "our" in prayer.

Think It Over

1. Who are some of the people I take with me into my "our" of prayer?
2. Who are some of the people I leave out?
3. How have my petty disagreements or deep antagonisms hindered my prayers?

In Other Words

"Let the Christian . . . conform his prayers to this rule in order that they may be in common and embrace all who are his brothers in Christ, not only those whom he at present sees and recognizes as such but all men who dwell on earth. For what God has determined concerning them is beyond our knowing except that it is no less godly than humane to wish and hope the best for them."

—John Calvin, *Institutes of the Christian Religion,* 3.20.38

Live It Out

When you pray today, say something like "Dear *Abba* of Jonathan and Jeannette" (Jeannette is my wife). Or "Dear Father of Ben, Joanna, and Sam" (our children).

Mention by name some of the people you have brought with you into your prayer closet. Obviously you can't name everyone, but you can at least name the ones that come to mind.

As you continue to practice saying *Abba*, whenever you see or talk to someone else, particularly those who may be troublesome or unknown, say, "Our *Abba*."

In Heaven 3

"But our citizenship is in heaven. And we eagerly await a Savior from there, the Lord Jesus Christ."

—Philippians 3:20

Jesus teaches his disciples to pray to our *Abba* "in heaven." What does that mean? And why does Jesus want us to utter that one little phrase among the precious few words of this prayer?

Is it to remind us that God is so far away, so much beyond our world? To remind us of the distance between ourselves and the almighty God of the universe?

Heaven is one of the most misunderstood words in the Bible. Just as we talk about our Father in heaven, so we talk about going to heaven when we die. We think of heaven, whatever that might be like, as our final destination.

But that's not the way the Bible speaks of heaven. Yes, it is the "place" where God dwells. Yet it is not a place of infinite distance but rather of infinite possibilities. Heaven is the control tower of the universe, the Oval Office of the cosmos. We tend to think of it as beyond the farthest galaxies, but it may be much closer than we imagine. Perhaps we could think of heaven not so much as a place as another dimension of reality. We can't see heaven, but it's as real as the subatomic world of quantum physics.

When Jesus ascends to heaven (Acts 1:6-11), he's not getting away from all the trouble on earth. He goes there to reign at the Father's right hand. The Bible promises that in the end, it's not so much that we will go to heaven, but that heaven will come to earth. Paul says, "We eagerly await a savior from [heaven]." And in God's final act of salvation, the "new Jerusalem"—the heavenly city—comes down from heaven and God makes his home among us here (Rev. 21:2-3).

> **Word Alert**
>
> ***Quantum physics*** **or quantum mechanics is (to put it all too simply) the study of the relationship between energy and matter. We can't typically see the effects of quantum mechanics with our eyes, but those effects are observable at the atomic and subatomic levels. Similarly, there is an unseen spiritual reality called heaven that pervades the universe.**

"Our citizenship is in heaven," says Paul. That doesn't just mean "this world is not my home, I'm just a-passin' through," as the old song says. It means we belong to the Father who is in heaven. We are citizens of God's heavenly kingdom, and we trust that in the end God will reign over all things in heaven *and* on earth.

Praying to our *Abba* in heaven is recognizing that no matter how bad, how tragic, how impossible, how difficult things look here in this world, and in our personal world, our *Abba*'s ear is tuned to our cries. He knows the end from the beginning. He has history in his almighty hands, and he will bring all things together in Jesus Christ.

In a poem commemorating a wonderful spring day, Robert Browning wrote, "God's in his heaven—all's right with the world." If we say that flippantly in the warm breeze and sunshine, it may seem like escapism. It may feel like telling someone who's suffering from cancer, "Don't worry: everything will be all right."

But trusting our *Abba* in heaven, it's absolutely and wonderfully true. God's in his heaven, and all *will* be right with the world.

There is no place in the universe beyond God's reach. No circumstance in our lives beyond God's control. No power in heaven or earth that is *not* beneath God's almighty hand. No unknown secret in our hearts. No need he does not understand. For he is our *Abba* in heaven.

Think It Over

1. How do you think of heaven? If you like to draw, sketch what you think it might look like. In what ways has this meditation challenged that view?
2. How does praying to the heavenly Father strengthen our prayers and our faith?
3. Picture your neighborhood when God comes to make his home among us. What will be different? Will anything stay the same?

In Other Words

"All shall be well, and all shall be well, and all manner of thing shall be well."

—Julian of Norwich

Live It Out

As you read the newspaper, watch the news, talk to friends, or struggle with your own difficult circumstances this week, remember that God is in control. Turn your concerns and worries over to the One who reigns in heaven.

4 Hallowed Be Your Name, Your Will Be Done . . .

"Therefore, since we are receiving a kingdom that cannot be shaken, let us be thankful, and so worship God acceptably with reverence and awe . . ."

—Hebrews 12:28

In *The Lion, the Witch, and the Wardrobe*, C.S. Lewis describes the first time the children hear about Aslan, who is a Christ-figure in the book:

> "Is—is he a man?" asked Lucy.
>
> "Aslan a man!" said Mr. Beaver sternly. "Certainly not. I tell you he is the King of the wood and the son of the great Emperor-beyond-the-Sea. Don't you know who is the King of the Beasts? Aslan is a Lion—*the* Lion, the great Lion."
>
> "Ooh!" said Susan, "I'd thought he was a man. Is he—quite safe? I shall feel rather nervous about meeting a lion."
>
> "That you will, dearie, and no mistake," said Mrs. Beaver; "if there's anyone who cannot appear before Aslan without their knees knocking, they're either braver than most or else just silly."
>
> "Then he isn't safe?" said Lucy.

> "Safe?" said Mr. Beaver. "Don't you hear what Mrs. Beaver tells you? Who said anything about safe? 'Course he isn't safe. But he's good. He's the King, I tell you."

He isn't safe, but he's good. That, in a nutshell, is the definition of holiness.

Immediately after the word *Abba* invites us into the intimacy of Jesus' own relationship with the Father, the first petition—"Hallowed be your name"—seems to fence us off.

But when we pray those words, we are praying for God to lift us up out of our deadly preoccupation with our own lives, to see God in his awesome holiness, to commit ourselves to his kingdom. Our *Abba* is also the infinite God of inexpressible mystery and blazing love.

"Your kingdom come, your will be done. . . ." You can't read very far in the gospels without realizing that Jesus' message was all about the kingdom of God. So it's not surprising to discover that the Disciples' Prayer is also a kingdom prayer. The very first thing Jesus teaches us to ask for is the coming of God's kingdom. And then he gives a sort of definition of that kingdom, "Your will be done on earth as it is in heaven."

The kingdom of God is the reign of God over all things. Jesus announces that God's kingdom has come near in him. God's kingdom will fully come when "every creature in heaven and on earth and under the earth and on the sea, and all that is in them" will sing "To him who sits on the throne and to the Lamb be praise and honor and glory and power, for ever and ever!" (Rev. 5:13).

Praying for the coming of God's kingdom means praying for God's will to be done. But praying for God's kingdom to come and God's will to be done is much more than a sort of wish that everything will come out all right. As Lucy learned, the kingdom isn't safe.

When we pray for the King to come, we invite him to do whatever he wants in and through us. If I pray for a hungry child in Darfur, for example, it would be irresponsible for me not to do anything as part of the answer to that prayer. Prayer isn't just leaving everything to God; it's more like becoming God's partner. Praying for God's kingdom and God's will pulls me into the orbit of God's grand purpose for creation.

And that brings us to another important aspect of the Disciples' Prayer: it's all about God. The prayer begins with a laser-like focus on who God is and what God is doing.

Notice that Jesus teaches us to pray "*your* name . . . *your* kingdom . . . *your* will." It's not *my* kingdom, *my* life, *my* little world. We need to be clear on this: prayer is not a means to our own ends. It's not a way to further our purposes.

Think of it this way. If you're coming in from fishing to land at the dock, you don't try to pull the shore to the boat, you pull the boat to the shore. In the prayer Jesus taught us, we are pulling our fragile bobbing craft to the great shore of God's kingdom, God's purposes, God's will.

Of course, Jesus does teach us to pray for our own needs in the next few phrases of the prayer. But we begin with what God is doing. When we start there, our prayers for our own needs become less selfish, wiser. We know better how

Reality Check

There are good and bad ways to bring the boat to the shore. In his early days of sailing, a friend once decided to put his foot on the dock as he was bringing the boat in. Somehow he ended up stretched out between the two with desperate determination, farther and farther, until he fell in the water.

to pray for ourselves when God is the beginning, the center, and the purpose of our lives.

When we pray "your kingdom come," we are praying for the King to come. We are asking Jesus to come and rule in the places we live and work and breathe.

The real question we need to answer now is this: Do we want the King around or not?

Think It Over

1. When you pray, "Your kingdom come, your will be done," what does the kingdom look like to you?
2. How does being a citizen of the kingdom affect the way you live? What risks do you feel called to take because of the King?
3. What difference does knowing that prayer is first of all about God make to your prayers?

In Other Words

"Perhaps you thought something like, 'Christianity is mostly a matter of trying to do the right thing and to live a good life.' But this way of viewing things gets the cart before the horse. Christianity is *not* mainly a matter of what we do or how we live, but first a matter of what God in Christ has done. We have no idea how to live until we first know who God is. So when we say that God's name is holy, that tells us how we ought to live. Knowing the Creator tells us where the creation is meant to move."

—William Willimon and Stanley Hauerwas, *Lord Teach Us: The Lord's Prayer and the Christian Life*

Live It Out

Try to repeat this crucial first petition from the Lord's Prayer through the day. See what difference it makes in how you live, how you think about your life. Does it affect what you read or see on the news? Your relationships?

Three Petitions 5

"Give us . . . Forgive us . . . Lead us . . ."

—Matthew 6:11-13

Give us, forgive us, and lead us. These three petitions of the Lord's Prayer, recorded in both Matthew and Luke and quoted by believers through the ages, cannot be described in a page or two. They must be lived into lifetimes.

They are petitions of provision, pardon, and protection that address our most basic human needs.

Give us this day our daily bread. "The problem in the Christian life," my friend Daniel Henderson tells me with a little bit of his tongue in cheek, "is that it is so *daily*."

Notice that Jesus in giving us the Disciples' Prayer doesn't have us say, "Give us this day our weekly or monthly paycheck." Or "Give us our seasonal harvest." Jesus wants us to pray for *daily* provisions.

Could Jesus' Jewish followers have heard this prayer and not thought of the manna in the wilderness? (Ex. 16). I don't think so. Certainly they would have been envisioning lessons learned over many years: bread that comes from heaven, that must be gathered and cannot be hoarded.

This is the prayer picture Jesus wants his disciples to have. We ask and he gives. We trust and he proves true. He provides and we gather.

And do you suppose that this might apply to more than just manna? Certainly this petitition is Jesus' invitation to pray for *Abba*'s provision over all of our lives. Give us this minute our breath. Give us every second our heartbeat. Give us our food and clothing, our housing and relationships. Give us what we need to live a full human life—nothing more and nothing less.

Forgive us our debts as we forgive our debtors. Some people pray "debts," some "trespasses," some "sins." That's because the two versions of the Lord's Prayer in Matthew and Luke use two different Greek words. In Matthew, the word most often means debt. In Luke the word is the more common one for sin—missing the mark.

Sin includes both of these senses. Sin is like a debt we've incurred to the righteous God, and it's missing the mark of God's perfect law. Either way, it's no surprise that one of the most basic human needs for which we pray is forgiveness.

What is surprising is the little phrase that Jesus tacks on to the prayer for forgiveness: "as we forgive our debtors." In Matthew's gospel, Jesus immediately follows the prayer with these words: "For if you forgive others when they sin against you, your heavenly Father will also forgive you. But if you do not . . . your Father will not forgive your sins" (Matt. 6:14-15).

Word Alert

The economic word *debtors* reminds us that debt forgiveness may extend beyond forgiving another's sins. For those who are in positions of economic power personally and globally, perhaps this prayer is also a call to debt forgiveness, or at least debt reduction in relation to the poor.

Does that mean God's forgiveness is conditional? Is it less than a free forgiveness? Maybe it's best to say that our forgiveness of others is not so much a *condition* of God's forgiveness as a *consequence* of it.

When we fail to forgive others, it shows that we do not understand or really accept the extravagant grace of our own forgiveness. Praying the Lord's Prayer reminds us that forgiveness is not only freely given *to* us but also that we are called to let it flow *through* us. We become part of the gravitational field of grace, transforming the enmity of this world into loving community.

Deliver us from evil. In his famous hymn, "A Mighty Fortress Is Our God," Martin Luther taught us to sing, "and though this world with devils filled should threaten to undo us . . ." And the apostle Paul writes, "Our struggle is not against flesh and blood, but against . . . the powers of this dark world and against the spiritual forces of evil" (Eph. 6:12).

It's a chilling thought. There are powers at work in this world and in our own hearts that loom over our lives like a dark shadow.

But these powers we sometimes call Satan, or the Devil, are not ultimate. Though far more powerful than we, they are under God's authority. As Luther concludes, "one little Word shall fell them." That Word is Jesus. Jesus Christ has won the victory over the powers of evil on the cross and triumphed over them in his resurrection. They are doomed.

So Jesus teaches us to pray for deliverance from evil, for divine protection from these powerful forces that stalk our path every day.

That doesn't mean we are granted immunity from their onslaughts, and it certainly doesn't mean we can play around with their tempting enticements. It does mean that we can live confidently in Christ's victory, declaring in his name, "Get behind me, Satan!" (Matt. 16:23). As John promises, "The one who is in you is greater than the one who is in the world" (1 John 4:4).

Think It Over

1. What do these three petitions teach us about praying for our needs?
2. What do you feel the most need for right now: provision, pardon, or protection? Freely, trustingly ask God for it today.
3. Do you need to forgive someone? Ask for God's transforming grace to flow through you.

In Other Words

"'Give' and 'forgive'—these are humanity's two great petitions of God. Please give us physically what we need in order to live like humans, then please forgive us spiritually those things that we do or don't do, in order to live free of guilt. . . . Please give us food so that we may stand up; please give us forgiveness so that we may stand up straight."

—Frederick Dale Bruner, *The Christbook*

Live It Out

As you go through each day this week, try to keep your commitment to the Father uppermost in your mind, "as I forgive my debtors." See how it affects your attitude and relationships.

The Great Addition
(A Brief Bonus Meditation)

"Yours, LORD, is the kingdom. . . ."
—1 Chronicles 29:11

If you read Luke 11 and Matthew 6 you probably noticed something missing. The Lord's Prayer as it has been used down through the ages includes a final stanza that is not included in either Matthew or Luke: "Yours is the kingdom and the power and the glory forever and ever. Amen."

The prayer starts out with "Thy kingdom come." So why would the church have chosen to include something in this prayer that was there already? Why mention the kingdom again?

And isn't it presumptuous for the church to include something in this prayer that Jesus doesn't include? Nowhere in the New Testament does Jesus tell the disciples to conclude their prayer with this last stanza, so why do it?

The Disciples' Prayer is a prayer prompt. Think of it this way: it's water to prime the pump, not the well itself. Jesus tells his disciples to pray "in this way" (Matt. 6:9, NRSV). He doesn't say "pray with these words and only these words." The Disciples' Prayer is not an incantation to be magically pronounced with supernatural results. It is more like an outline for a much larger and longer dialogue.

These closing words were added as early as the second century, and they form a fitting conclusion to the prayer. The prayer ends where it began, with its laser-like focus on God and God's kingdom. It guarantees that our prayers do not dribble away like a leaky faucet but end with bold confidence in God's kingdom, God's power, and God's glory.

In Other Words

"This is the firm and tranquil repose for our faith. For if our prayers were to be commended to God by our worth, who would ever dare even mutter in his presence? Now . . . we will yet never lack a reason to pray, never be shorn of assurance, since his Kingdom, power and glory can never be snatched away from our Father."

–John Calvin, *Institutes of the Christian Religion*, 30.20.47

Session 1
The Lord's Prayer
Discussion Guide

Prayer, the saying goes, is more caught than taught. Before the disciples asked Jesus to teach them, they watched him. They noticed the way Jesus prayed; they caught its intimacy, its power, and its unwavering centeredness on God.

So let's get started. Let's put on our headphones and listen to the language of prayer as Jesus speaks it for us. To put it another way, let's follow Jesus in the practice of prayer.

Ice Breakers

(15 minutes—give or take)

If this is a new group meeting for the first time, **take some time to get acquainted**. Distribute blank 3 x 5 cards and write down in bullet form five things about yourself that you don't mind others knowing about you. Have one person collect them and read them out loud to see if the group can guess who each card belongs to. Don't worry if you're new to the group—there's no winning or losing. The more you know about each other, the more everybody wins.

Option

If that seems too gimmicky, just go around the circle and introduce yourselves. Do include a brief, fun story of when you did something you really wished you hadn't done.

If this is a continuing group, take a few minutes to get reaquainted. **If there are any new members, everyone should briefly introduce**

themselves as in the option above. If not, invite group members to share their first prayer memory. Perhaps you have an early memory of sitting in a church service. Or maybe you remember devotions at the family table. How did you feel? What were you thinking? Take some time to share your "first words" or "first pictures" of prayer.

For Starters

(5 minutes)

Invite group members to briefly share one insight they gained from the devotional readings. Don't discuss it now, just mention it.

Let's Focus

(5 minutes)

Reread the introduction to these five sessions and then have someone read this focus statement aloud:

Prayer, at least for Jesus' followers, is caught before it is taught. When you take a close look at Jesus' life as portrayed in the gospel of Luke, you'll notice that it is shot through with prayer. Jesus is at prayer for his baptism, he spends all night in prayer before naming his disciples, and he struggles in prayer in the Garden of Gethsemane before the cross. In the prayer we call "the Lord's Prayer" (or the Disciples' Prayer) and throughout his life, Jesus taught us how important prayer is. The Lord's Prayer isn't our only prayer, but it is Jesus' own model for how we should pray.

Word Search

(20 minutes)

Discuss the following Scripture passages (or, if you're running short on time, choose the ones the group wants to discuss):

- Romans 8:14-17
  What is the spirit of slavery and fear Paul is referring to?

Who enables us to cry *Abba!* Father?

What does addressing God as *Abba* signify to us?

How does the "our" of Jesus' prayer broaden this intimate name of God?

- Luke 17:20-21
  What does Jesus mean that the coming of the kingdom of God is "not something that can be observed?"

  What does it mean that it is "in your midst"? How does this color the way you pray "Your kingdom come, your will be done"?

- Matthew 18:21-35
  Why is Jesus so insistent on our forgiving others?

  Why can't the unforgiving be forgiven themselves?

An Encouraging Word

Some people have been deeply harmed by the sins of others (think of those whose lives have been turned upside-down by abuse, betrayal, divorce, murder). For some of these people, forgiveness may be more like a process than like a momentary act. Praying this petition of the Lord's Prayer serves as a constant reminder of the journey of forgiveness they're on, and of the Savior's love and strength that will enable them to arrive. If this is an issue for you, make sure to check the website for more resources: www.GrowDisciples.org.

In Other Words

"Why should you fear? Why should you be afraid? Do you not know that the prince of this world has been judged? He is no lord, no prince any more. You have a different, a stronger Lord, Christ, who has overcome and bound him. Therefore let the prince and god of this world look sour, bare his teeth, make a great noise, threaten, and act in an unmannerly way; he can do no more than a bad dog on a chain, which may bark, run here and there, and tear at the chain. . . . Therefore everything depends on this, that we do not feel secure but continue in the fear of God and in prayer; then the chained dog cannot harm us."

—Martin Luther

- Ephesians 6:10-20
  What do you think Paul means when he says that "our struggle is not against flesh and blood, but against . . . the powers of this dark world and against the spiritual forces of evil . . ." (v. 12). How have you experienced this reality?

  Paul caps this passage with a call to prayer (vv. 18-20). Why is prayer the ultimate weapon against the overwhelming forces of evil?

Bring It Home

(20 minutes, or as time allows)

Choose *one* of the following options.

Option 1

Work together as a group to **create a banner or wall hanging that pictures or illustrates the Lord's Prayer.** You may use words, but don't forget symbols, pictures, or even abstract designs. Draw it on a sheet of newsprint. Maybe someone will want to put it on fabric or PowerPoint for the worship space.

Option 2

As time permits, choose from among the following questions and discuss them:

- Invite the members of the group to share together one aspect of their study of the Lord's Prayer that has impacted their thinking about and practice of prayer the most. Take the time to discuss.
- Do you include the Lord's Prayer in your prayers? If so, how? Does your church include the prayer in worship? When and how often? Does your study of it this past week change your ideas about how to use this prayer personally or corporately?
- How does the fact that the Lord's Prayer is so "God-centered" affect your prayer life and what you seek in prayer?

Option 3

Jesus was the master teacher who taught the disciples how to pray. Do you know other "teachers" of prayer—people whose godly lives reflect a close walk with their *Abba*? Maybe that person is your mom or dad, a godly grandparent, a dear friend. Take the opportunity to **share how these teachers have influenced your own prayer life, and thank God for them!**

Pray It Through

(10 minutes)

Take time to suggest items to pray about together.

You might want to begin your prayer by trying one-word prayers, perhaps just one adjective that characterizes your relationship with God (mysterious, kind, loving, remote, or whatever). Don't make it "spiritual"—make it personal and make sure each person in the group has several chances to speak out a word. If that seems too threatening for your group, list some of the words on a 3 x 5 card and share it with one person of your choosing from the group.

Alternatively, use the phrases of the Lord's Prayer as prayer starters. One person says, "Our Father in heaven . . ."; the other group members have an opportunity to offer brief words, phrases, or prayers to fill out that phrase for them personally. Continue with "Hallowed be your name . . . ," and so on.

Live It Out

(5-15 minutes each day during the coming week)

Praying the Lord's Prayer is an opportunity to deepen your relationship with your *Abba.* It is also an invitation for the King to work in

Web Alert

You'll want to check out the participants' section for this session on www.GrowDisciples.org for tips, interesting links, and suggestions for follow-up reading for this session.

your life. Are you ready for that? Spend some time thinking about some of the ways you might need to step out of your comfort zone to allow God to use you for the coming of the kingdom. Then look for ways to follow God's prompting as you pray the prayer Jesus taught. Be prepared to share some of these next week with the rest of the group.

Session 2
Trinitarian Prayer

fourteenth-century icon of the Holy Trinity by Andrei Rublev. This icon recalls the story of Abraham's three
ngelic visitors (Gen. 18) as a symbol of the Trinity.

Father 1

"Our Father in heaven . . ."

—Matthew 6:9

"All things have been committed to me by my Father. No one knows who the Son is except the Father, and no one knows who the Father is except the Son and those to whom the Son chooses to reveal him."

—Luke 10:22

Trinity. Most Christians shy away from thinking too much about this seemingly abstract and complicated doctrine. One God, three persons . . . our heads start to spin. Yet the Trinity is absolutely fundamental to the Christian faith. Without it, we would simply not be Christians.

The early church leaders didn't develop this doctrine because they wanted to get all philosophical about God. They simply couldn't avoid it because they bumped up against it in the very language the New Testament uses about God. Almost from the beginning, we meet God as Father, Son, and Holy Spirit.

It's right there in the prayer Jesus taught us: "Our Father . . ." For Jesus to address God as Father, he must recognize himself as the Son. We call God our Father because we know him as Father through Jesus the Son. Jesus is the Son who was sent to make the Father known.

This father/son language isn't about assigning gender, as we mentioned last week. It's about relationship. Father and Son are the way Jesus reveals to us the deep mystery of the inner relationship of persons in the very being of God. It's something like the relationship of a human father and a son—except it's a perfect relationship. By using these terms God is speaking our language.

Christian prayer, like the Christian faith in general, is trinitarian. The Bible teaches us that prayer is addressed *to* the Father, *through* the Son, *in* the Holy Spirit. It's a conversation with the One who is above us as Creator, beside us as Redeemer, and in us as Sustainer.

The conversation doesn't begin with us. It's a conversation that's been going on from eternity, but we're invited to join in when Jesus invites us to pray to the Father.

Imagine this. You're observing a family engaged in animated conversation. It's obvious that what they're talking about is very important and that they love each other very much. Their faces reflect the flow of the conversation—from smiles of delight to worried frowns to eager anticipation.

You're an outsider, an observer, but you also feel very drawn to what's happening. You sense the bonds of love and commitment that tie the family together.

Now imagine that one of them sees you standing across the room and invites you to join the conversation. You feel shy about entering so intimate a relationship as a pure stranger. You try to decline, but the oldest son, who is an acquaintance, insists. Come over here; join us. And soon you're in on the whole family business.

That's something like the way prayer draws us into the very inner life of the triune God, the eternal loving relationship of the three persons within the Trinity. Through prayer we become part of the family.

Jesus is the one who invites us into that conversation of holy love. He's the Son who took on our full human life, who became one of us and still continued his eternal conversation with the One he called *Abba*.

And now, especially because he died and rose again to reconcile us to God, he brings us into the family. We become adopted sons and daughters by baptism, and we can now cry *Abba*, Father (Rom. 8:15). We're in on the family business of the kingdom of God.

And that's why Christians pray in Jesus' name. He's the one who brought us into a relationship with his *Abba.*

Think It Over

1. In what ways is your father on earth like your Father in heaven? In what ways different? How do the similarities and differences affect your prayer life?
2. What does it mean to you that your prayer is part of a much bigger conversation?

In Other Words

"Calling God 'Father' is the great act of faith, of holy boldness, of risk. Saying 'our Father' isn't just the boldness, the sheer cheek, of walking into the presence of the living and almighty God and saying, 'Hi, Dad.' It is the boldness, the sheer total risk of saying quietly, 'Please may I, too, be considered an apprentice son.' It means signing on for the Kingdom of God."

—N. T. Wright, *The Lord and His Prayer*

Live It Out

Do you know someone who's standing outside but maybe looking in at the warmth of your church family? Practice Jesus' hospitality by inviting that person to come on in and join the conversation about faith. Go out for coffee, or better yet, invite this person to your home for a meal. Invite her to attend a worship service with you, and offer to pick her up.

The Name of Jesus 2

"Very truly I tell you, all who have faith in me will do the works I have been doing, and they will do even greater things than these, because I am going to the Father. And I will do whatever you ask in my name, so that the Father may be glorified in the Son. You may ask me for anything in my name, and I will do it."

—John 14:12-14

My dear children, I write this to you so that you will not sin. But if anybody does sin, we have an advocate with the Father—Jesus Christ, the Righteous One."

—1 John 2:1

Some people are shameless name-droppers. "I got a call from Ms. Local Celebrity today." "My friend Joe Famous dropped in for coffee last week."

In a way, Christians are name-droppers too. We drop the name of Jesus in at the end of all our prayers. Why do we do that? Sometimes it seems like a mere form, a way to draw the prayer to a close, like ending a conversation with, "See you later."

But there's an important reason why we speak the name of Jesus at the end of our prayers: it's a powerful name that opens up a whole world of possibilities.

The author of the book of Acts invokes the name of Jesus time after time. In the name of Jesus the apostles promise forgiveness of sins (Acts 2:38). In the name of Jesus they offer healing (3:6, 16), cast out demons (16:18; 19:13), and encourage one another in the face of persecution (21:13). But most important of all, "There is no other name given under heaven by which we must be saved" (4:12). Only Jesus' name can save us.

Jesus' name doesn't have magical powers, it has relational powers. There is power in the name we proclaim because there is a person behind the name, and he stands behind his name. That person is Jesus, and he's our brother.

But there's another reason why we use the name of Jesus in our prayers. He's our *advocate* with the Father.

A woman once had to appear in court to straighten out a legal matter in relation to Social Security. She happened to have a friend who was one of the most well-known and widely respected lawyers in the city. People with cases before an administrative law judge are seldom represented by a lawyer—much less a really good one. So you can imagine how the judge's jaw dropped as this prestigious attorney strode into the room.

We all need an advocate who will stand up

Word Alert

The Greek word for advocate is *paracletos*. It means someone who pleads another's cause before a judge, a pleader, counsel for defense, or legal assistant. In the New Testament both Jesus and the Holy Spirit are called advocates. The Spirit advocates for us by teaching us the truth and purifying our prayers. The Son advocates by pleading our cause.

for us. The Bible calls Jesus our advocate. He lived a perfect and wonderful human life for us. He died on the cross for our sins and failures, and he rose again to give us eternal life in him.

Afterward he ascended to the Father, and now he stands before the God of heaven and earth and intercedes for us. As our representative, he says to the Father, "These are my brothers and sisters for whom I was sent, for whom I died. When you think of them, think of me. When you look at their lives, look at mine. They are mine."

That's the ultimate reason why we pray "in Jesus' name." We pray in the name of the One who purchased us by his own death and resurrection, whose name is written all over us in our baptism.

The book of Hebrews calls Jesus the high priest who represents us in heaven. So when we come into God's own holy presence, we do so with confidence in our advocate the High Priest.

Think It Over

1. How might understanding and trusting in the power of Jesus affect how you pray?
2. Think of a situation in which you needed an advocate. How did it feel to have someone "in your court"? What difference does it make to know that Jesus is your advocate when you confess your sins in prayer?

In Other Words

"Praying in Jesus' name . . . means sensing a oneness with the Lord as his sister or brother. It is a recognition that only through him is the believer able to have access to the Father. It means sharing in Jesus' certainty of being heard. The believer knows that the Father hears, because God is being approached through the Son, Jesus."

—Stanley J. Grenz, *Prayer: The Cry for the Kingdom*

Live It Out

Throughout this week, whenever you find yourself feeling helpless before some problem, or guilty for some sin, speak the powerful name of Jesus. Remember that he is your advocate who represents you with his own life and love before the Father.

Spirit 3

"In the same way, the Spirit helps us in our weakness. We do not know what we ought to pray for, but the Spirit himself intercedes for us through wordless groans. And he who searches our hearts knows the mind of the Spirit, because the Spirit intercedes for God's people in accordance with the will of God."

—Romans 8:26-27

Christians have sometimes been accused of constructing an alternative Trinity: Father, Son, and "Holy Scriptures." Like me, you may come from home or habits that give some truth to that jest. With the exception of the Pentecostals, who emphasize living in the power of the Holy Spirit, most of us have a lot to learn about living in the Spirit's power and by the Spirit's influence.

Both Matthew and Luke conclude Jesus' teaching on the "Disciples' Prayer" with his encouragement to us to *ask*. Matthew records Jesus encouraging us to ask for good gifts: "If you, then, though you are evil, know how to give good gifts to your children, how much more will your Father in heaven give good gifts to those who ask him!" (Matt. 7:11). Luke emphasizes asking for *the gift*, "If you then, though you are evil, know how to give good gifts to your children, how much more will your Father in heaven give the Holy

Spirit to those who ask him!" (Luke 11:13). It seems that if you have the Spirit, you really need little else.

My dear wife is teaching me about asking. She believes in what Jack Canfield calls "The Aladdin Factor." We go to a restaurant. We sit down. We don't like our seats. I accept our spot in silence, but she asks, "Could we sit in a booth instead?" When the dinner is poorly prepared, I eat, but she asks, "Could you cook this a little more?" We talk and eat better in restaurants because Jeannette asks.

Jeannette also teaches me about prayer. As a pastor, I tend to start speaking before I start asking. She, on the other hand, is not used to public speaking and praying. She has learned before she prays in public to ask specifically that the Holy Spirit will give her the right words. And it works!

Like Jeannette, we all need help in our prayers. Paul honestly acknowledges that fact: "We do not know what to pray for." Or, as another translation has it, "We do not know how to pray as we ought." I know that and you know that, but to recognize that God knows it *and* provides an answer is wonderfully comforting!

The Spirit helps us. How? Again we step into the holy ground of the trinitarian mystery. The Spirit knows our deepest and truest longings better than we do. God the Holy Spirit lives within us and has access to our deepest desires.

God the Spirit and God the Father are of one mind, and so the Spirit interprets our mixed-up, unformed thoughts and desires and turns them into what we "ought to pray." The Spirit, who understands our hearts' desires even better than we do, purifies our prayers and passes them along to the Father.

That doesn't mean we just stop praying and let the Spirit do it for us. All parents long to hear the delightful babblings of their two-year-old.

God wants to hear our every stammering word. At the same time God hears the interpretation of the Spirit who helps us to pray.

Is something missing in your prayer life? Ask for help.

We expect our prayers to come naturally. But the Bible reminds us that no one is a "natural" at prayer. We need the Spirit's help.

Contrary to conventional wisdom, God doesn't "help those who help themselves." The oldest Reformed liturgy always began with the words, "Our help is in the name of the Lord who made heaven and earth." We *start* our worship with a reminder that we need help, and that's the way we start our personal prayers too.

The venerable and wonderfully personal Heidelberg Catechism, written in the sixteenth century, asks, "Why do Christians need to pray?" The answer? "Because God gives his grace and Holy Spirit only to those who pray . . . asking God for these gifts and thanking him for them."

There's one thing you can ask for in your prayers that you will always receive—the Holy Spirit. God wants to send his Spirit more and more fully into your heart and soul. God wants you to be part of the family and to enter deeply into the family conversation.

Word Alert

A *catechism* is a summary of Christian teaching, typically in the form of questions and answers. One of the most well-known catechism questions in the Heidelberg is the first: "What is your only comfort in life and death?" The answer: "That I am not my own, but belong—body and soul, in life and in death—to my faithful Savior Jesus Christ." Another memorable question and answer begins the Westminster Shorter Catechism: "What is the chief end of man?" "To love God and enjoy him forever." You might want to memorize these!

Think It Over

1. What are your struggles in prayer?
2. How does the Holy Spirit's indwelling and praying presence help you pray with more confidence?

In Other Words

Eternal Spirit of the living Christ,
I know not how to ask or what to say;
I only know my need, as deep as life,
and only you can teach me how to pray.

Come, pray in me the prayer I need this day;
help me to see your purpose and your will
where I have failed, what I have done amiss;
held in forgiving love, let me be still.

—Words: Frank von Christierson, Words © 1974 The Hymn Society (admin. by Hope Publishing Co., Carol Stream, IL 60188). All rights reserved. Used by permission. Permission to reproduce this text must be obtained from Hope Publishing Co., www.hopepublishing.com.

Live It Out

Try the following "breath prayer" today. Take a deep breath; while the air is coming into your mouth say the words "Fill me with your Spirit." As you exhale, say the words "Forgive me for my sins." As you breathe in, imagine the new life brought by the oxygen of God's grace and mercy freshly flowing through your body. As you exhale, imagine all the carbon dioxide of your own sin leaving your body for good.

The Conversation of Creation 4

"In the beginning God created the heavens and the earth. Now the earth was formless and empty, darkness was over the surface of the deep, and the Spirit of God was hovering over the waters. And God said . . ."

—Genesis 1:1-3

Words create. Conversation creates. At least that is what the book of Genesis suggests. God doesn't *think* creation into being. He doesn't even *act* it into being. He *speaks* it into being.

Who is God talking to when he is manufacturing the universe? Could God be talking to himself? Sometimes when I'm working on a project alone, I talk myself through the steps: "OK, first I've got to get the hammer and stud finder. . . ."

But the creation story reveals a different pattern. Creation isn't a solitary act. There are other Persons around.

Think of it this way. If God were talking to himself, wouldn't he say, "Let *me* make humans in my own image"? Instead, we hear God say, "Let *us* make human beings in our own image." This is more than just a "royal we"—the way the British queen speaks in plural rather than singular. This is a plural "us."

In Genesis we get our first glimpse of the three-personed God . . . and they are talking to *each other*. They are, in a sense, praying. God says, "Let there be light . . ." and there is! God says, "Let there be fish . . ." and there are! God creates through the Word—"Through him all things were made" (John 1:3)—with the breath of the Spirit.

How did I come into the world? I believe it was my mom and dad saying to God in prayer the equivalent of, "Let there be Jonathan." Children are brought into this world through prayer. Try to convince me that Jonathan Edwards or Billy Graham weren't prayed into place, not just by parents, but by a great throng of people praying for revival and renewal!

What about you? Could you be the answer to prayers other than those of your parents? What might you do with your life? What kinds of prayers might you be an answer for? I know of several parents who pray for their children's future spouse. Could it be that those prayers started to be answered before that future spouse was born?

Prayer is the conversation of creation. And as surely as God said, "Let us make . . ." and it was so, we are invited to participate in God's work of creation through our prayers.

"Then God said, 'Let us make human beings in our image, in our likeness, so that they may rule over the fish of the sea and the birds in the sky, over the livestock and all the wild animals, and over all the creatures that move along the ground.' So God created human beings in his own image, in the image of God he created them; male and female he created them. God blessed them and said to them, 'Be fruitful and increase in number; fill the earth and subdue it. Rule over the fish in the sea and the birds in the sky and over every living creature that moves on the ground.' . . . And it was so. God saw all that he had made, and it was very good.

And there was evening, and there was morning—the sixth day" (Gen. 1:26-28, 30b-31).

We exercise dominion—not by domination but by caring intercession. As a friend of mine likes to say, "Intercessors rule the world." Not politicians but pray-ers. Those who pray in the name of the Father, Son, and Holy Spirit turn the clock back to Genesis and create.

Instead of "And God said," could it be "and Jonathan prayed"? When I or any follower of Jesus speaks in his name, something is created. Prayer looks over the chaos of the world today, over its formless and empty places, and brings out of it God's beautiful purposes.

"Let there be light in Holland, Michigan," a group of pastors says every Thursday morning as we gather together to pray. God hears our prayers and something is created in the city—maybe a child is born or maybe a person's hope is reborn. One thing is certain: something changes when we converse with the Creator. Behold, it is very good to pray. You might call it a good day's work.

Wouldn't you like to be a part of *that* kind of prayer? When we enter into the conversation of creation, understanding and embracing the triune God in all God's glory, we're taking a step in the right direction.

Think It Over

1. In what sense are your prayers part of God's creative work?
2. If you believed that every time you talked to God some wonderful purpose was born, would it change how you prayed? What would you pray for?

In Other Words

"[Praying for God's kingdom] is adding one's own soul-force to the cosmic struggle of the love of God against the powers of darkness."

—Charles Elliot, quoted in John Koening, *Rediscovering New Testament Prayer*

Live It Out

For the next seven days, structure your prayer as suggested here to remind you that you are continuing the conversation of creation:

"And [*your name*] says, let there be [*add your request: healing for a loved one, hope for elderly parents, an end to violence in your city or neighborhood, and so on*]."

The Recipe of Revelation 5

"When all the people were being baptized, Jesus was baptized too. And as he was praying, heaven was opened and the Holy Spirit descended on him in bodily form like a dove. And a voice came from heaven: "You are my Son, whom I love; with you I am well pleased."

—Luke 3:21-22

What happens when Jesus prays? You could answer that question a hundred different ways, couldn't you? A herd of pigs jumps off a cliff (Mark 5:1-14). A blind beggar receives his sight (Luke 18:35-42). A tax collector vows to repay all the people he's cheated (Luke 19:1-8). Lots of things happen when Jesus prays.

Here's another question: What happens when Jesus prays before and during his baptism? Three things.

First, Jesus' prayer opens the heavens.

The Bible mentions other occasions when the heavens are opened. Check out Genesis 7:11, for example: "In the six hundredth year of Noah's life, on the seventeenth day of the second month—on that day all the springs of the great deep burst forth, and the floodgates of the heavens were opened." During the flood, the heavens open and rain floods the earth. On that occasion, the heavens open in judgment.

For Jesus' baptism, however, the heavens are opened not for rain but for revelation. The sun breaks through the clouds so that the Son is revealed. But that wasn't the first occasion on which the Bible describes such a revelation. Consider the following passages:

- "In the thirtieth year, in the fourth month on the fifth day, while I was among the exiles by the Kebar River, the heavens were opened and I saw visions of God" (Ezek. 1:1).
- "About noon the following day as they were on their journey and approaching the city, Peter went up on the roof to pray. He became hungry and wanted something to eat, and while the meal was being prepared, he fell into a trance. He saw heaven opened . . ." (Acts 10:9-11).

Prayer not only creates; it also illuminates. We see more when we close our eyes to pray!

Second, Jesus' prayer brings down the Spirit.

Yesterday's reading considered the creation account in Genesis; today we read the account of Jesus' baptism. Notice that both accounts feature a Spirit hovering over the water . . . and what is it that sets the Spirit in motion? It is prayer.

Jesus' prayer brings the Spirit down on him—"in bodily form like a dove." In the Old Testament, Samuel's prayer brought the Spirit down on David, symbolized by the oil: "So Samuel took the horn of oil and anointed him in the presence of his brothers, and from that day on the Spirit of the Lord came upon David in power" (1 Sam. 16:13).

Third, Jesus' prayer amplifies a voice from heaven.

Not only is prayer the conversation of creation, it is the recipe of revelation. It illuminates and it amplifies. When we join the triune conversation, we have the opportunity to bring new things to life. We also have the opportunity to redeem old things for a better life.

We receive power from a hovering Spirit, we are given direction through a voice from heaven, and we are changed.

Should we expect to see God when we pray? Yes! Should we expect to hear God when we pray? Yes!

Let me be more specific. When we pray we will see manifestations of God. We will see God working and moving in extraordinary ways—in the words of the prophet Joel, we will see "wonders in the heavens and on the earth" (Joel 2:30).

Will we hear God? Certainly. Will that voice from heaven be audible? Perhaps. More likely though, God's voice will speak to us through circumstances and senses. We will know in our hearts what God wants us to do, whether it is carried through our eardrums or not.

Think It Over

1. What do you think Jesus was praying about before his baptism?
2. What are some of the ways you've heard God speaking to you when you've prayed for God's guidance or direction?
3. What "signs and wonders" have you seen that display God's presence and power?

In Other Words

"[Prayer] has as its goal the altering of life situations."

—Stanly J. Grenz, *Prayer: The Cry for the Kingdom*

Live It Out

This week in your prayers boldly ask God to open the heavens, send down his Spirit, and speak. Prepare to see God working in your life in amazing and unexpected ways.

Session 2
Trinitarian Prayer
Discussion Guide

We won't keep talking to someone for very long if we don't know who he or she is. In fact, my rule of thumb with sales pitches over the phone is, if I don't know you or the product you represent, you will get a polite "no thank you" and then a dial tone.

Christians believe that we can know God—not because we are particularly smart, but because God is wonderfully gracious. We know because God shows. We comprehend because God comes. He is Immanuel, God with us; God up close and personal.

We describe that up-close and personal God with a rather distant and theological term: the Trinity. We tend to focus on head knowledge rather than heart or hands. We use nouns rather than verbs to describe the character of God.

Nouns tend to distance and dispassion God. Verbs, on the other hand, can help bring God up close and in person. Let me illustrate:

- The Father loves.
- The Son saves.
- The Holy Spirit empowers.

If we don't know someone well, we sometimes describe them by what they do. Who is your mail carrier? She's the one who puts the mail in my box every day. Who is your cousin? I can't remember his name, but I think he's the one who lives in Tucson, Arizona.

To be honest, we don't know God all that well. He is so much beyond our comprehension. The Trinity does not contain or fully describe God. It is just a start. Who is God? I don't fully know, but I believe God is the one who loves me as a parent loves. God is also the one who sent his Son to save me.

The Apostles' Creed is the universal creed of the Christian church. It includes the words, "I believe in the Father . . . in Jesus Christ, his only Son, our Lord . . . in the Holy Spirit." That's who God is.

Our surprising discovery this week is that the doctrine of the Trinity has enormous and very practical implications for how we pray.

Word Alert

The word *Trinity* comes from two words: *tri* and *unity*—literally, three persons united. God is not just a person, but a community for all eternity. Through Jesus, the Son, we are invited into this community right now. Prayer is the language of this community.

For Starters

(5 minutes)

Invite members of the group to share one insight, surprise, or question they had from the devotional readings. Don't discuss it right now, simply mention it and what it meant to you.

Let's Focus

(5 minutes)

Read the introduction and then have someone read this focus statement aloud:

We pray to the Father through the Son in the Holy Spirit. Prayer is more than just a way of talking to God; it's a way of entering into a conversation that takes place in the loving fellowship of the Trinity for all eternity. Jesus introduces us to the Father as his *Abba.* Now the Father is our *Abba* too—by dying and rising again, Jesus opened the way for us to become adopted sons and daughters of the Father. But we don't know that until the Father sends his Spirit into our hearts at Jesus' request. The Holy

Spirit inspires us to cry *Abba* with trust and confidence. So in prayer we enter into the very life and fellowship of the holy Trinity!

Word Search

(15 minutes)

Read aloud the following Scripture passages and briefly discuss the question under each one (or formulate a better one of your own).

- Ephesians 3:14-19
  What do you think Paul means by describing God as the Father "from whom every family in heaven and on earth derives its name"?

  How does this prayer model for us the way in which prayer is our communion with the Holy Trinity?

  What is the special role of each person of the Trinity in this prayer?

- John 14:15-17, 25-26
  Identify and discuss the role of each person of the Trinity in Jesus' comforting words.

  What does this teach us about prayer?

Bring It Home

(20 minutes)

Choose *one* of these options:

Option 1

Invite each group member to **make a simple line drawing or diagram on a piece of paper that depicts how we are involved with the whole Trinity through prayer.** Make sure to include yourself somewhere in the diagram. **Share the results with the group.** Or work on this together as a group on your board or on sheets of newsprint.

Option 2

As time permits, **discuss some or all of the following questions together as a group.** Or use this time to discuss any other questions that came up as you reflected on the readings for the week.

- Have you thought very much about the Trinity until now? Has it seemed more like an abstract doctrine or a living reality in your life?
- We began by saying that we pray to the Father through the Son in the Holy Spirit. Does that mean we should never pray to Jesus or the Holy Spirit? Why or why not? *Hint:* There's a difference between a guideline and a rule!
- How do we enter into the "conversation" that's already going on between the Father, Son, and Holy Spirit in our prayers? In what way does that comfort us and encourage us to pray?

Option 3

Provide each group member with a ball of modeling clay or Play-Doh and invite everyone to figure out a way to **shape their clay into a symbol of the Trinity. Share the clay sculptures with each other,** and explain your symbol to the rest of the group. Keep them out as reminders of how we participate in the fellowship of the Father, Son, and Holy Spirit in our prayers.

Pray It Through

(10 minutes)

Take time to suggest items to pray about together. These may be items of praise, thanksgiving, confession, or petition, or they may be related to the issues raised by this session. Because we have explored how prayer is deeply trinitarian this week, you might begin the prayer by asking someone to say the names *Abba* (Father), Lord Jesus, and Holy Spirit, pausing after each name to allow a few moments for group members to offer words of praise. Pray in whatever way your group feels most comfortable: one or more persons praying, popcorn style, or each member praying for the person on the right or left.

Live It Out

(Each day during the coming week)

One of the daily readings describes prayer as "a good day's work." That's because entering into the conversation of prayer really makes a difference in our lives and in our world. Each day think of a specific situation that you can lift up in your prayer conversation: your brother-in-law's search for meaningful employment, a loved one's health concern, or the well-being of your neighborhood, for example. Thank your *Abba* for hearing your prayers in the name of Jesus, our Lord, through the power of the Holy Spirit.

Web Alert

Be sure to check out the participants' section for this session on www.GrowDisciples.org for interesting links and suggestions for readings and activities that will deepen your understanding and experience of praying in communion with the Trinity.

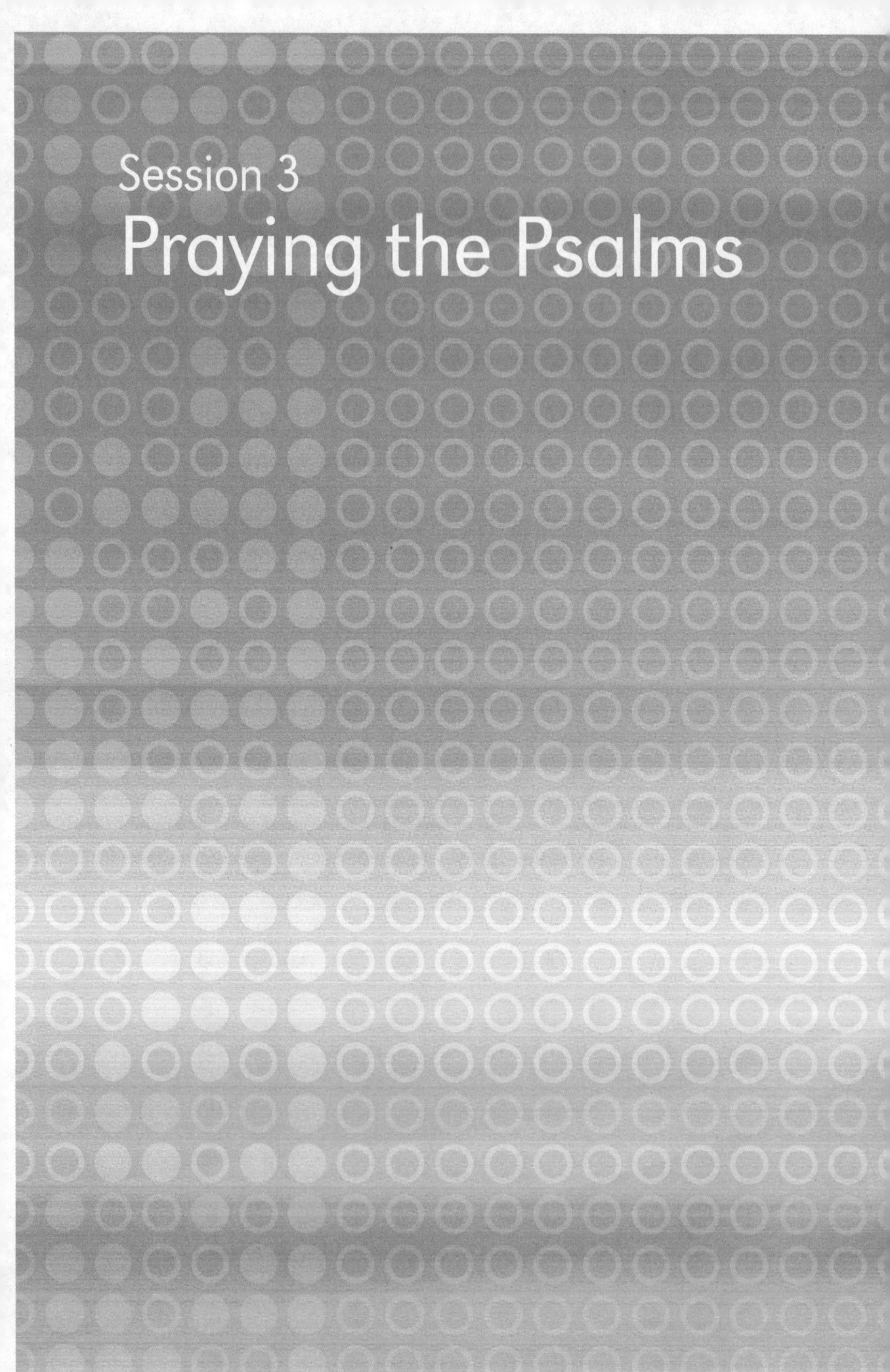

Session 3

Praying the Psalms

The Bible's Own Prayer Book 1

"I will exalt you, Lord, for you lifted me out of the depths and did not let my enemies gloat over me. Lord my God, I called to you for help, and you healed me.

—Psalm 30:1-2

Can you guess who's speaking in the following story?

I'm twelve years old and back in school after a vacation. When the teacher asks, "What did you do on your break?" I tell him, "We went to the same place we go every year. It's 81 miles away and since we don't have a car, we walk. We pack up most of what we own, put it on the backs of a few animals, and then head out. We go as far as we can, and at the end of the day we stop and pitch a tent. Then we start again early the next morning until we get there. When we arrive in the city we buy a lamb. Then we go to church and kill it. Then we turn around and start the long trip home. Oh yeah, while we hike, we sometimes sing.

Helpful Hint

Since we are exploring the Psalms as our primary school of prayer this week, why not read the whole psalm with each meditation this week?

That's right—it's Jesus in one of the rare glimpses we get of his early life (see Luke 2:41-52). Every faithful Jewish family took an annual journey to Jerusalem for the Passover, and on the way they sang to keep up their spirits as they walked.

What did the people of Israel sing? They sang Psalms 120-134, also called the Songs of Ascent. That's because Jerusalem was built on a hill, so they were actually going "up" to the house of the Lord (Ps. 122:4).

About the only traveling song I can remember is "Ninety-nine bottles of beer on the wall." We'd sing it on the bus on our way back from athletic events, at least until we got bored or the coach stopped us.

The Israelites didn't have hymnals. They had to carry these songs in their hearts because they couldn't carry anything else on their backs. Most Jews committed the Psalms to memory from childhood. That's one of the reasons the Psalms are the most quoted part of the Old Testament in the New Testament. Jesus and Paul and Peter knew them, and they just flowed out of their hearts.

Word Alert

A *hymnal* is a collection of psalms and hymns used by the church for worship. It often contains creeds and doctrinal confessions as well; together these represent the prayer and praise of God's people of every age and from many places.

But the Psalms are more that just traveling songs. They're used for worship and for private prayer. They are poems of praise and prayers of sadness, even angry letters to God. In fact, you will find nearly every human thought, emotion, and desire expressed somewhere in this amazing book.

From the beginning, Christians have recognized the importance of the Psalms for their prayer and worship. Jesus prayed the Psalms all his life and likely knew them all by heart. In fact, Jesus prayed them on the cross. Many of the famous "seven last words" from the cross are actually words and phrases from the Psalms.

Paul calls on Christians to sing "psalms, hymns and songs from the Spirit" (Eph. 5:19). In the fourth century, Benedict, the founder of the monastic movement, built the whole day around seven times of prayer in which all the psalms were prayed during each twenty-four-hour period, a practice that continues in many monasteries today.

At the time of the Reformation, John Calvin and other reformers insisted that the psalms were the *only* songs congregations should use in worship because they are from the Spirit-inspired Bible. (That practice continues in some Reformed churches.) And even the songs used in "contemporary" worship today are often based on or use phrases from the Psalms (for example, the much-loved *Shout to the Lord,* Psalm 100:1). The point is, Christians have always recognized the special place of the Psalms in shaping their prayers and their worship. It's truly the "prayer book of the Bible."

During this week, we'll explore how the Psalms can help us learn how to pray and how we can use them as our prayers, just as we might use the Lord's Prayer. That's what disciples of Jesus do.

The Lord's Prayer introduces us to the relationship with *Abba* that makes prayer possible. The Psalms teach us how to pray in and through all the circumstances of our lives.

Think It Over

1. Have you thought of the Psalms as your prayer book, and as the prayer book of the church?
2. Do you know any psalms by heart? What are they, and when did you learn them?

In Other Words

"The Psalms are the best tools available for working the faith—one hundred and fifty carefully crafted prayers. . . . People of faith take possession of the Psalms with the same attitude and for the same reason gardeners gather up rake and hoe on their way to the vegetable patch. . . . It is a simple matter of practicality—acquiring the tools for carrying out the human work at hand."

—Eugene Petersen, *Answering God*

Live It Out

Incorporate a verse from a psalm into your heart this week by memorizing it. One good way to do this is to make it a part of your exercise routine: whenever you're climbing the stairs or walking to the office or taking a morning run, repeat a verse or even a single phrase.

Praise 2

"Praise the LORD. . . . Great are the works of the LORD; they are pondered by all who delight in them. Glorious and majestic are his deeds, and his righteousness endures forever. He has caused his wonders to be remembered; the Lord is gracious and compassionate."

—Psalm 111:1-4

Some of us were taught an excellent method called ACTS to guide our prayers: Adoration, Confession, Thanksgiving, Supplication (petition).

For some folks, the hardest part is Adoration. I don't know exactly why. We find it easy to praise the smart coaching and last-minute play that won the playoff game. It comes naturally to recommend the great movie we saw last week. But when it comes to praising God, we're often tongue-tied. Or reduced to the stock phrase "Let's just praise the Lord."

Could it be that we find it hard to express our adoration because God's power and greatness are not immediate in our everyday experience? Or do we feel inadequate to the task because praising God is like giving an adequate description of a spectacular mountain valley or of the heart-stopping moment you first fell in love? It takes a poet to do that. We can't seem to find the words—certainly not on the spot.

And because we're at a loss for words, this is one of the most splendid ways the Psalms help us to pray. They put words in our mouths! Maybe that idea doesn't seem so splendid—maybe it strikes you as sneaky or dishonest. We generally resist people putting words in our mouths because, well, they're not our words, our thoughts.

But like the hymns in our hymnals or the words of a song projected on the screen in worship, the Psalms are *meant* to put words in our mouths. They help us offer praise to God in language saturated with awe, beauty, reverence, and joy. The Psalms give us poetic license to praise God in the most lovely, imaginative, and soaring words.

God is a shepherd, a fortress, a shelter, a light, a rock. The Lord is enthroned over all, his covenant lasts forever, he cares for the poor and defenseless, he walks with me through the shadow of death. The lightening flashes, the seas roar, the mountains smoke. All creation shouts its praise: sea monsters, fruit trees, shining stars, kings of the earth. This is expansive, heart-pounding, mind-bending praise. And it's ours to pray.

Which brings up another question: Why? The Psalms are always urging us to praise the Lord, to magnify his name, extol his mighty works. Does God need our praise? Is God waiting to be told how great he is? That can't be!

Praise is not for God, it's for us. There's something about praising God that completes us and makes us whole. It's the best and grandest thing we humans can do before our Creator, Savior, and Sustainer.

We know that from experience. If you've ever traveled alone, you've probably discovered that in one way it can be unsatisfying. When you see or experience something really great, you need to tell someone. Wasn't that mountain grand? Can you believe that gorgeous palace?

That's also why it feels so good to be part of a great crowd roaring its hurrahs after a spectacular slam dunk, or rising to its feet at the close of a thrilling concert. We need to praise because it completes our enjoyment.

Most of all we need to praise God because God is the greatest imaginable being whose mighty acts are beyond description. The book of Psalms closes with a symphony of praise that throbs with rhythmic joy (Ps. 150):

> Praise the LORD. . . . Praise him for his acts of power; praise him for his surpassing greatness. Praise him with the sounding of the trumpet, praise him with the harp and lyre, praise him with timbrel and dancing, praise him with the strings and pipe, praise him with the clash of cymbals, praise him with resounding cymbals. Let everything that has breath praise the LORD.

Can you imagine how grand it will be at last to join with the whole creation singing, roaring, and shouting our praise and adoration to the living God? After all, it's what we were made for, as the Westminster Shorter Catechism puts it: "to glorify God and enjoy him forever."

We can practice today and every day with the God-inspired words of praise offered to us in the Psalms.

Think It Over

1. Do you find it easy or difficult to offer praise to God? Why?
2. What have been the most satisfying moments of praise for you?

In Other Words

"To see what [praise] really means we must suppose ourselves to be in perfect love with God—drunk with, drowned in, dissolved by, that delight which . . . flows out from us incessantly . . . in effortless and perfect expression. . . ."

—C. S. Lewis, *Reflections on the Psalms*

Live It Out

Pray Psalm 145 today. Take note of the particular expressions of praise that especially stir your heart.

Passion 3

"My God, my God, why have you forsaken me?"

—Psalm 22:1

Some people have a hard time showing emotion. So do some Christians. We may have come from a tradition that was pretty buttoned-down emotionally. We may have associated dignified, staid prayer, especially in worship, with reverence. Such prayer was not emotional—and certainly not in a way anyone could see it on the outside.

As the Bible's prayer book, the Psalms teach us something different. Prayer involves our whole being: our mind, our bodies, and our emotions. The Psalms address them all. There are acrostic poems for the mind and enough wisdom for a lifetime. There's music and dancing for the body. And there's just about every kind of emotion people experience—despair and rage as well as joy—right there out in the open. And it's all expressed to God!

Emotions are almost impossible to suppress or deny. They will come out—in ways that are either appropriate and helpful or inappropriate and unhelpful. Bottle up your emotions too

Word Alert

Psalm 119, the longest psalm, is an *acrostic*. Each stanza begins with a letter of the Hebrew alphabet, and each line in that stanza begins with that same letter. Imagine combining a love of Scrabble, Sudoku, or crosswords into composing a prayer!

long and they're likely to explode the way a can of Coke explodes after you shake it. They are part of how God made us.

The Psalms take human emotions seriously as an essential part of being human. There's everything from "make a joyful noise to the Lord," to "my tears have been my food day and night."

Many Christians associate the Psalms with the positive emotions of joy and praise. We aren't as comfortable with the many psalms that express negative emotions. Yet here's where they can be most helpful. Every feeling—really, every one—is expressed to God in psalms. Anger, jealousy, fear, disappointment, despair, revenge, bitterness—it's all there, and more.

Here's the point: we have all these feelings, whether or not we want to admit it. Should we somehow hide them from God? We can't, so why try? The best thing is to be real in our prayers, to say what we really feel, even when it's despair or hatefulness or fuming anger.

There is a difference between taking God's name in vain and taking God's name in pain. God will never turn away anyone who takes his name in pain. Pathos (deep feelings) he understands. Apathy God will not abide: "Because you are lukewarm—neither hot nor cold—I am about to spit you out of my mouth" (Rev. 3:16).

God can handle our human emotions, even when we're angry at him, and even when we can't handle them very well ourselves, especially when we don't bring them before the light of God's presence.

Psalm 88 is so emotionally wrenching that it begins in despair and darkness and ends there too, without a single word of hope. Yet it's a prayer addressed to God.

On the cross, jeering crowds below, pain wracking his body, and darkness all around, Jesus prayed the opening words of Psalm 22, "My God, my God, why have you forsaken me?" This Psalm Jesus had learned as a boy gave him the words he needed to pray in the dark on Golgotha.

And maybe Jesus kept praying that psalm he knew so well by heart all the way through to the end:

> Revere him all you descendants of Israel! For he has not despised or scorned the suffering of the afflicted one; he has not hidden his face from him but has listened to his cry for help (vv. 23b-24).

When we pray the Psalms, whether with words of praise or passion, we are praying them with Jesus. He came to be our brother, God as a human being. As our brother he took up every hurt, every pain, every insult, every feeling, every temptation we experience.

Think It Over

1. What emotions do you feel comfortable expressing in prayer?
2. Does it seem right to you to express disappointment or even anger at God?

In Other Words

"I have been accustomed to call this book . . . 'An Anatomy of all the Parts of the Soul'; for there is not an emotion of which any one can be conscious that is not here represented as in a mirror. Or rather, the Holy Spirit has here drawn to the life all the griefs, sorrows, fears, doubts, hopes, cares, perplexities, in short, all the distracting emotions with which the minds of men are wont to be agitated."

—John Calvin, *Commentary on Psalms*

Live It Out

Pray Psalm 55, a prayer of anguish in time of trial and betrayal. Think of Jesus in the Garden of Gethsemane, betrayed by Judas, abandoned by his other disciples. Can you pray it with Jesus? How does it also connect with your life?

Penitence 4

"Have mercy on me, O God, according to your unfailing love; according to your great compassion blot out my transgressions. Wash away all my iniquity and cleanse me from my sin."

—Psalm 51:1-2

I am at a Life Action Ministries gathering in Overisel Reformed Church in Michigan. Seven area churches have committed to meeting every night of the week for ten days straight.

Tonight's speaker hands out a "Bible mark." It is a bookmark for a Bible, a resource to be used for daily devotions. You've probably seen them: "How to pray for your pastor," "Prayers for the local church," and so on. This particular Bible mark has the title "How to have a holy hour" and it says that a "holy hour" starts with confession.

That's true also when we pray the Psalms. We don't pray psalms just because they are soothing, or comforting, or because they sound beautiful either to us or to God (even though they are). We pray them because they are beautifully searching, honest prayers from the heart.

If we simply mouth the words, we're likely to be misled by the devil. However, if we pray the words with broken hearts, then we will find forgiveness and fresh hope.

If we leave confession out, we invite deception in. And God wants honest prayer. Holy hours start with confession . . . but how? The Psalms put words of confession in our mouths in the seven "penitential psalms" scattered throughout the book.

The psalm that helps me do that best is Psalm 51. Have you ever prayed it? Better yet, have you memorized it?

Word Alert

Psalms 6, 32, 38, 51, 102, 130, 143 are called the *penitential psalms*. A penitent is one who expresses sorrow for wrongdoing. Prisons came to be called *penitentiaries* in the nineteenth century because there a criminal would supposedly come to terms with his or her wrongdoing. The penitential psalms are touching, probing, painful expressions of the many ways in which sin hurts us, each other, and God. But instead of imprisoning us in the penitentiary of our guilt, they free us to confidently trust in God's forgiveness.

The heading (very early on the Jewish "editors" of the Psalms assigned some of them to various events in David's life) says that David prayed this psalm after committing adultery with Bathsheba. You may remember how the prophet Nathan tells a story about stealing to David and then says to his enraged listener, *"You are the man."* (Read the shocking story for yourself in 2 Samuel 11.)

Nathan could have just as easily said to me, "You are the man!" And before you agree too quickly, let me say, he could have said the same to you. We all desperately need to pray Psalm 51.

I have been praying Psalm 51 with the encouragement of my Bible mark regularly. I don't always have holy hours, but often when I pray its words, I have convicting moments.

"Cleanse me with hyssop. . . ." I remember seeing the plant hyssop near En Gedi in Israel. Our travel guide told me that when the juice is extracted from the plant it has about the same corrosive qualities as battery acid. Wash me in battery acid. Scrub me with Comet cleanser, if that is what it takes for me to be pure and pleasing in your sight.

"Against you, you only, have I sinned. . . ." True confession isn't vague or general, it's personal. I feel the pain of hurting or disappointing others whom I love. Then I realize that every sin against God's created ones is a sin against the Creator. What I have done—or failed to do—to the least of these, I have done to him. All our sin is a personal affront to God.

"My sacrifice, O God, is a broken spirit; a broken and contrite heart you, God, will not despise. . . ." How comforting that I find God's promised presence in that place I most fear: the place of brokenness, failure, and sin. If I dare to go there, letting the laser beam of God's holiness shine on my dark, shadowy heart, God will be there with his grace.

Think It Over

How can the penitential psalms enable us to confess our sins with greater honesty, understanding, and grace-filled gratitude?

In Other Words

"Who we are—not who we want to be—is the only offering we have to give. We give God therefore not just our strengths but also our weaknesses, not just our giftedness but also our brokenness. Our duplicity, our lust, our narcissism, our sloth—all are laid on the altar of sacrifice."

—Richard J. Foster, *Prayer*

Live It Out

For the next few days, take time to examine your heart to see what sin or sins the Holy Spirit might bring to your mind. Then pray one of the penitential psalms each day, and see how they expand your sense of both sinfulness and grace.

Ugly Prayer 5

"Break the teeth in their mouths, O God; Lord, tear out the fangs of those lions! Let them vanish like water that flows away; when they draw the bow, let their arrows fall short. May they be like a slug that melts away as it moves along, like a stillborn child that never sees the sun. . . . The righteous will be glad when they are avenged, when they dip their feet in the blood of the wicked. Then people will say, 'Surely the righteous still are rewarded; surely there is a God who judges the earth.'"

—Psalm 58: 6-8, 10-11

How does a Christian pray these words and others like them? After all, these verses are not an isolated case but a regular sentiment found throughout the Psalms, and this example is far from the most brutal.

One of the most troublesome feelings Christians have to deal with is anger at the injustices, insults, and crimes visited on us and upon others. We hear of a terrible crime—a rape, a murder perhaps—and it's hard not to think along the lines of these verses from Psalm 58. We read of the horrors visited upon innocent people by the tyrants of the world, and we want to see them pay dearly for their atrocities.

The fact that these kinds of feelings are openly expressed in the Psalms is disturbing and, I hope we can also see, helpful. Don't get me wrong. These Psalms of rage and vengeance don't provide us an example of how we should act toward our enemies. Jesus' words "Love your enemies and pray for those who persecute you" (Matt. 5:44) are still true. But getting there is not a simple decision, and it doesn't eradicate the feelings we have on the way.

The Psalms give voice to all our feelings, even the most horrible ones. When we pray with the psalmists for vengeance, when we join them in spilling our guts in anger, we are bringing those dark and dangerous emotions into the only safe place to express them—before God.

There's no point in denying them or stuffing them down. We know they're there, and certainly God knows too. The Psalms teach us to pray them, to bring the feelings we harbor in the darkness into the light of God.

One interesting aspect of these ugly prayers is that they do teach us an important truth about ourselves and God. Paul says, quoting Deuteronomy, "'It is mine to avenge; I will repay,' says the Lord" (Rom. 12:19). There is judgment. The unrepentant wicked will pay for their crimes and atrocities. But we do not do it. Only God has the wisdom, truth, and understanding to mete out righteous judgment.

As far as I can tell, every one of the so-called "imprecatory" psalms, psalms of vengeance, call upon God to do just that. They're not justifications for personal vengeance, they're prayers for God to do what is right.

But what about praying these psalms when everything in your life is going just fine? I don't have any enemies, I don't harbor feelings of anger or vengeance. This brings up an aspect of praying not just these dark psalms, but any psalm that expresses feelings we can't identify with directly at the time. I'm not depressed, or in deep trouble, or beset by enemies. Why should I pray this way?

Word Alert

***Imprecatory* is the adjective of *imprecation*, which means to invoke evil upon, to curse. It's the term biblical scholars use for this particular type of psalm. Imprecatory psalms are an important part of the vocabulary of prayer not only because they express our real feelings but, even more important, because they express the hope for God to do justice.**

Here's the secret. Like the Lord's Prayer with its constant "our," we join with the whole Christian community when we pray the Psalms. I might not be depressed, but perhaps I know someone who is. I certainly know that some brother or sister is in a very dark place today. So I pray with them and for them.

Praying these psalms reminds me that even when my life is going just fine, many of my brothers and sisters are hurting, persecuted, oppressed. It puts me in the middle of the whole messed-up world we live in. I can't avoid it or ignore its troubles and pains.

These psalms we'd like to avoid are also gifts from God. They teach us how to pray and give us the words—even sometimes words we hesitate to place on our tongue.

Think It Over

1. How do you feel about these kinds of psalms and their sentiments? How have you dealt with them in the past?

2. Have you ever heard one of these psalms said or sung in worship? How did that help or hinder your worship?

In Other Words

"Hate is our emotional link with the spirituality of evil. It is the volcanic eruption of outrage when the holiness of being, ours or another's, has been violated. . . . This hate arises in the context of holiness: meditating on the holy word of God, expecting the holy messiah of God."

—Eugene Peterson, *Answering God*

Live It Out

Try praying the whole of Psalm 58 or another of the imprecatory psalms with the principles we've discussed in mind.

Session 3
Praying the Psalms
Discussion Guide

Our son Sam is a songwriter. He shared with us one of his songs the other day and we cried. Sons are not necessarily supposed to make parents cry—but songs are. He told us that our tears were one of the greatest compliments we could have given him as a songwriter.

The Psalms are songs that make us feel—maybe more accurately they are songs that help us to express our feelings. They're like floodgates for our emotions. The Psalms are our language of prayer. Think of it this way: if the Disciples' Prayer is *first* words, the Psalms are *felt* words. The Psalms are both prayer and poetry.

They are our language of license, words that are intended to set us free, not enslave us; not stumble over them but swim in them. They are an ocean to carry us, not a straightjacket to limit us. In the very beginning was the Word, and so words are the things that create.

The Psalms do more than make us feel, they help us express what we feel toward God. They give both freedom and focus to our feelings. They give entrée to a conversation with God. I believe that is why Paul both in Ephesians and Colossians specifically tells the church to use the Psalms: "[Speak] to one another with psalms, hymns and songs from the Spirit. Sing

Word Alert

As *poetry* the Psalms do not have the same kinds of rhythm or rhyme we expect. Nor are they just "free verse" with little structure. One of the characteristic features of Hebrew poetry is *parallelism*. One line repeats the same thought but in different words: for example, "Do you rulers indeed speak justly? Do you judge people with equity?" (Ps. 58:1). Once you get the idea, you'll notice this pattern all over the Psalms.

and make music from your heart to the Lord. . . ." (Eph. 5:19). "Let the message of Christ dwell among you richly as you teach and admonish one another with all wisdom through psalms, hymns and songs from the Spirit, singing to God with gratitude in your hearts" (Col. 3:16).

Sam is a songwriter. David is too. Will you let King David share some of his songs with you? Will you let them move you? Cry and cry out with them. Laugh and let go with them. Ask questions and argue with them. And when the tears come, let's together break the alabaster jar at the feet of Jesus.

For Starters

(10 minutes)

Invite group members to share one insight, surprise, or question from the devotional readings. Don't discuss it now, just mention it and what it meant to you.

Let's Focus

(5 minutes)

Read the introduction to this session; then have someone read this focus statement aloud:

The Psalms offer us a treasure trove of prayers that both teach us how to pray and give us the words we can use in prayer. They cover the entire gamut of human emotion. Some soar with high praise. Some dare to express our darkest thoughts. Some offer wisdom by which we can live. It's clear from Jesus' life recorded in the gospels that the Psalms were often on his lips, and we can pray them with him.

> Word Alert
>
> ***Gamut* comes from the medieval musical scale (like our *do, re, mi, fa, so, la, ti, do*—like Julie Andrews sang in *The Sound of Music*). *Gamma* was the first note; *ut*, the second, all shortened to gamut. It's come to mean the full range, like the whole scale of human emotions.**

Word Search

(20 minutes)

Read aloud the following Scripture passages and briefly discuss at least some of the questions under each one (or formulate a better one of your own).

- Psalm 57

  What do the introductory words say about the setting of the psalm, and how it might have been used? (The introductory words were not original to the Psalms but added later by their users and other editors of the collection.)

  How does this psalm demonstrate some of the characteristics of the Psalms we've been considering this week? How might it be helpful to think of praying this psalm with Jesus?

- Psalm 27

  Invite each group member to pick out their favorite verse or phrase from this beloved psalm and tell why. Perhaps some have had an experience in which this psalm, or a part of it, became a prayer of their heart. Invite them to share it.

Bring It Home

(15 minutes)

Choose one of these options:

Option 1

Write a short psalm of your own. You could do this together as a whole group, or divide into smaller groups, or work individually. It may be a psalm of praise, lament, or penitence. Try to incorporate the parallelism so typical of the Psalms (see Word Alert, p. 95), and use your own poetic devices. Then share your psalms together.

Option 2

Discuss *some* of these questions as time allows. Or take up a problem or question group members highlighted earlier from the devotional readings.

- What do you find most difficult about reading or praying the Psalms?
- What is most helpful or rewarding about praying the Psalms?
- What new ways have you discovered this week to help make the Psalms part of your prayer life?
- Why do you think that the early Church Fathers and the Reformers believed the Psalms were so essential to prayer that they made them the backbone of all their prayer and public worship? Would that be desirable today?

Option 3

If someone has a guitar or other instrument, plan to **sing some psalms as a group.**

Pray It Through

(10 minutes)

After your usual sharing of prayer concerns and thankgiving, close your session by praying a psalm together. (It may help to have a single version of the psalm printed and copied for all the participants.)

Live It Out

Start a practice of praying the Psalms that corresponds to the day of the month. For example, if today is the first of the month, today you would read Psalm 1. Or just start praying the Psalms in order. You will be surprised to see how this prayer practice works in your soul over time.

Web Alert

Be sure to check out the participants' section for this session on www.GrowDisciples.org for interesting links and suggestions for readings and activities.

Session 4

The Problems of Prayer

PUSH
FOR
COIN

Unanswered 1

"He withdrew about a stone's throw beyond them, knelt down and prayed, 'Father, if you are willing, take this cup from me; yet not my will, but yours be done.' An angel from heaven appeared to him and strengthened him."

—Luke 22:41-43

Simple requests don't always have simple answers.

A son asks, "Mom, can you get me a drink of water?" No response. He tries again: "MOM, I'm thirsty!" Again, no response. "MOM!!"

In the best of all worlds, a mother will answer her son's request with a drink of water. But we are not in the best of all worlds. Sin creates static. What if the water her son seeks is laced with arsenic? Or what if her son is not the only one who is thirsty? What if a whole village is without water and there are others who need it more?

Here's the reality: what God intended to be casual conversation in the Garden of Eden has become sweat-soaked groaning in the Garden of Gethsemane. Even though God is willing and able, sometimes God "cannot" answer . . . or at least God does not answer the way we want.

Jesus is the perfect Son. He has never done anything to disappoint his Dad. During his whole life, he has rarely asked anything for himself. Now, in an hour of deep need, he asks, "Take this cup from me." Jesus is talking about a "cup" of intense suffering he is about to endure. He is looking for some way to avoid being killed on a cross for the sin of the world.

If Jesus doesn't always get what he asks for in his prayers, will we? If you were to listen in on some of my prayers, here's what you might hear: "Father, if you are willing, take the brain damage caused by encephalitis away from my brother Billy. Father, if you are willing, take the schizophrenia away from my next-oldest brother David."

God hasn't done either of those things. As one song puts it, "You can't always get what you want." In our fallen world, we don't always get what we ask for.

One problem is our vantage point. We simply don't know God's grand purposes and how our lives fit into them. British pastor and theologian P. T. Forsyth put it well: "We shall come one day to a heaven where we shall gratefully know that God's great refusals were sometimes the true answers to our truest prayer" (quoted by Richard Foster, *Prayer*). Our distance vision as finite human beings is hardly 20/20.

Then again, sometimes our prayers are answered, but we can't see it. God's ways are mysterious, and they may sometimes escape our notice. God's answers may not be exactly what we asked for, but they are exactly what we needed.

So what do we do when we don't get an answer? We keep on asking. We hit "redial" or send another e-mail or post another Facebook entry. When we really need an answer, we keep on asking!

Jesus tells two stories about people who "keep on asking" in the gospel of Luke. In the first (11:5-8), a man knocks on his friend's door in the middle of the night because he has unexpected company and no food to serve them. He doesn't necessarily want to keep on knocking, but he has no other choice. In the second story (18:1-8), a woman comes to a judge to request justice. At first he ignores her but she persists until finally he gives in—he wants to be rid of her constant nagging.

Some answers to our prayers are almost instant—we ask to find our lost keys and the next place we turn they suddenly "appear." Others, however, outlast a lifetime. Think of the Old Testament people profiled in Hebrews 11, what some have called the "Hall of Faith" chapter—Noah, Abraham, Moses, Rahab, and others. All of them prayed for deliverance. But God's answer—a Messiah who delivers the world from sin and death—does not come until after they die!

These men and women of faith are assured of what they hope for and convinced about what they cannot see. So they keep on asking until they can't ask anymore. Sound familiar?

Think of the Garden of Gethsemane. Think of Golgotha.

We know someone, don't we, who prays until he dies. Suffocating under the weight of our sin, stretched out on a cross, Jesus keeps asking for an answer. He prays Psalm 22 until he can't pray—can't breathe—any longer: *Eloi, Eloi, lema sabachthani?*

Jesus keeps on praying in the face of unanswered prayer. And he tells us to do the same: "Always pray and [do] not give up" (Luke 18:1).

Word Alert

Golgotha **is Aramaic for skull. It was the name of a hill outside Jerusalem where Jesus was crucified, so called, apparently, because its form resembled a skull.**

Think It Over

1. Do you ever get discouraged by unanswered prayer? How do you deal with it?
2. Have you ever stopped praying for something after a while? In what ways might that be an appropriate response or a faithless response?

In Other Words

"One of the least-heralded truths among people of faith is that when they pray regularly and repeatedly for something to happen, it often does."

—John Koenig, *Rediscovering New Testament Prayer*

Live It Out

Keep a record of your prayer requests this week, and make a list of answered prayers and those that are not answered (prayers for peace, healing for a friend who has cancer, and so on). Ask the Spirit to give you the discernment to recognize the prayers God has answered and the faith to trust God when your prayers seem to go unanswered.

Undisciplined 2

"Then [Jesus] returned to his disciples and found them sleeping. 'Couldn't you men keep watch with me for one hour?' he asked Peter. 'Watch and pray so that you will not fall into temptation. The spirit is willing but the flesh is weak.'"

—Matthew 26:40-41

Sometimes God doesn't seem to answer. Sometimes we don't bother to ask.

It's 11:00 p.m. They are in the same bed. The wife is talking. The husband is snoring. *Jonathan, could you not listen to me for one minute?* I admit that there have been rare moments in our marriage when I have fallen asleep in the middle of a conversation with my wife. My spirit has been willing, but my flesh is weak.

How about you? Are you willing and weak sometimes when it comes to prayer? Does your heart get ahead of your habits? Do you sometimes find it hard not only to close your eyes in prayer, but also to keep them open?

Jesus never intended to "come to the Garden alone," in the words of the old gospel song. He wants his followers with him in prayer. He has been praying *for* them, and now he wants them to start praying *with* him. As Jesus faces his most critical hour, he longs for the partnering prayers of his followers.

> **Word Alert**
>
> **A *spiritual discipline* is a regular practice that enables us to live in loving relationship with God and our neighbor.**

Prayer is a spiritual discipline (notice the close connection between the words *discipline* and *disciple*). There are all kinds of these disciplines—worship, Bible reading, fasting, giving—but certainly one of the top disciplines for disciples is prayer.

The word *discipline* sounds heavy. It suggests duty more than desire. It's surrounded by "shoulds" and "oughts." So for many Christians prayer goes hand in hand with guilt—"I don't pray like I should."

That's unfortunate, because no real spiritual growth comes out of guilt. Besides, it's not as though God is poised with a clipboard counting the hours and minutes. Perhaps it may help to realize that prayer isn't for God—it's for us. If we don't pray, we lose out on the love, intimacy, hope, endurance, faith, and power that come from regular prayer. And, as Jesus points out, regular prayer is essential if we're to overcome temptation.

In fact, most of the good things in our lives require some discipline, some persistence, some habit. Think of prayer as a sort of spiritual hygiene. Heart and vascular health demands some kind of regular exercise. And just as you wouldn't go through a day without brushing your teeth, good spiritual hygiene requires daily prayer.

Some disciplines are easier than others. Brushing our teeth, for most people, is an easier discipline to establish than daily exercise. And for many Christians, daily prayer is not an easy discipline to establish. As Jesus said to his sleepy disciples, "The spirit is willing but the flesh is weak."

Why is that? Perhaps because we know that prayer *will* draw us closer to God. It *will* open our ears to Christ's call to be his disciples. Let's face it—we're not always sure we want to go there. Resistance to prayer is part of our sinful state. We love God, but there's a natural drag that keeps us from getting too close. We want to keep our lives for ourselves.

So how can we build regular, daily prayer into our lives?

First, we need to get rid of the notion that it's an obligation we owe to God and realize that it's a discipline we need for our own spiritual health and growth. In other words, we need to recognize that guilt doesn't work as motivation.

Second, if you really have a hard time with this, start small. Maybe it's saying the Lord's Prayer when you get up or go to bed. Maybe it's one minute of asking God for help and strength for the day to come. Anything to get started in a regular way. Remember, God's not counting the minutes, he's happy to have you in touch.

Finally, recognize that we are all different, and we all pray differently. For some, silence is golden; for others a list of "prayer concerns" really helps; for still others, a prayer book with a liturgy of prayer works best. It's not so important *how* you pray—that may depend more on personality and circumstances. What's important is *that* you pray regularly.

Web Alert

Be sure to check this session at www.growdisciples.org for lots of helpful articles, websites, and other resources on prayer.

Think It Over

1. How's your spiritual hygiene regarding prayer? What part, if any, does guilt play in the struggle?
2. Do you really want to pray regularly? Why or why not?

In Other Words

"To pray is to change. Prayer is the central avenue God uses to transform us. If we are unwilling to change, we will abandon prayer as a noticeable characteristic of our lives. The closer we come to the heartbeat of God the more we see our need and the more we desire to be conformed to Christ."

—Richard J. Foster, *Celebration of Discipline*

Live It Out

Ask God to help you improve your spiritual hygiene this week. Choose one small step—maybe, as the author suggests, it's praying the Lord's Prayer daily or beginning each day with a short prayer for help and strength. Maybe it's turning off the iPod while you walk the dog and paying attention to what's going on around you. Lift up your prayer as you walk!

Predestination 3

"In love [God] predestined us for adoption to sonship through Jesus Christ, in accordance with his pleasure and will—to the praise of his glorious grace, which he has freely given us in the One he loves. . . . In him we were also chosen, having been predestined according to the plan of him who works out everything in conformity with the purpose of his will. . . . For this reason, ever since I heard about your faith in the Lord Jesus and your love for all his people, I have not stopped giving thanks for you, remembering you in my prayers."

—Ephesians 1:5-6, 11, 15-16

She knew.

She had dreamed about it even before they spent much time together. There were other dates with other people. Still, she knew the day would come when he would bend his knee and say, "Will you marry me"? She knew she would.

Is it a problem that she knows? Not for her future husband. This is the foreknowledge of a future partner. She knows that the marriage is "predestined in love." For someone else, though, the whole scenario could look pretty strange. How does she know he is going to ask? And if she knows what he is going to ask and when, why would he even bother?

There is mystery in the way love works. It both *lets* things happen and *makes* things happen.

Paul believed that before the beginning of time God knew that he would knock him off his horse, blind him with the truth, and send him out to the ends of the earth with the gospel. God knows what he will do and when he will do it.

Still, at the end of Paul's long description of God's predestination, Paul *prays*. This doesn't seem logical. Why ask God to do something (or not do something) when God has already predetermined it? Or why would Jesus say, "Your Father knows what you need before you ask him" (Matt. 6:8) and then teach his disciples the Lord's Prayer?

Word Alert

***Predestination* is one of the words the Bible uses to describe the fact that God doesn't wait around for things to happen. God has determined to redeem the world in his Son, and to have a people who are transformed to be like Jesus. For us it means that we, along with God's creation, have a *destiny*, a good one, and that's very comforting.**

Paul prays because he believes God predestines in love. Paul understands that the loving God desires our willing participation in all he determines to do. Even though God, like the woman expecting her engagement, knows what is going to happen, he still wants us to be part of making it happen.

Think of Christ and the church, bridegroom and bride as described in Ephesians 5:25ff. There is a wedding planned at great cost! Still, in the mystery of mercy, the wedding can't happen without the Bride—the church. Love can't grow unless both bride and groom participate in the process.

God's part is predestination—his eternal purpose to have a people who are "conformed to the image of his Son" (Rom. 8:29). The church's part is prayer. God knows and does everything, but he knows and does everything at our request. God may have ultimate control, but he chooses to act with our consultation and cooperation.

Does an all-knowing Groom *desire* our prayers? Yes. He doesn't have to include us in his plans, but he does. God doesn't want puppets, but partners. God knows what is going to happen, but he also wants us to ask it into being. For a logician that doesn't make sense. For a lover it does. God wants to be in a relationship with us, but he will not force a proposal on us. God freely gives to us so we will freely give back.

Does an all-powerful Groom *need* our prayers? If God could set galaxies in place without us, place more stars in the sky than the sand on a seashore, why would God need us? Who are human beings that God cares for us? (Ps. 8:4).

We are talking here about love. God not only wants our partnership in prayer, he ordains the necessity of it. He predestines prayer into the mix. God is always looking for willing, prayerful partners in the ongoing work of his kingdom.

Think of a father who wants the grass to be mown. He knows the lawn will be cut one way or another. But he decides in advance that it will be cut with his son's help so he teaches him how to do it. Love looks for a co-laborer.

Why take the time? God could have tended the garden himself. Instead God gives the dominion, the work of the world, to us. The Father has determined that we will join him in mowing the lawn—caring for and governing the earth. Christ the bridegroom has determined to see us washed with "water and the word," walking down the aisle of history, spotless. Still, God seeks us out as his bridal partners in prayer and work.

By the amazing logic of God's determined, predestining love, nothing of significance will happen in this world unless we ask. So let's get busy!

Think It Over

1. Has the thought that God's plan is already determined hindered your prayers?
2. In what ways has this meditation helped you reconcile the seemingly illogical pairing of prayer and predestination?

In Other Words

"God takes immediate cognizance . . . of man's prayer in His governance of the world. Something does take place as a result of man's prayer, which otherwise would not take place. In fact . . . man's prayer is one of the most effective means by which God directs the world forward towards its goal, the Kingdom of God."

—Otto Hallesby, *Prayer*

Live It Out

Think of something that you know is God's will for you or for others and pray for it confidently with all your heart this week.

Hypocrites and Pontificators 4

"And when you pray, you must not be like the hypocrites, for they love to pray standing in the synagogues and on the street corners to be seen by others. Truly I tell you, they have received their reward in full. But when you pray, go into your room, close the door and pray to your Father, who is unseen. Then your Father, who sees what is done in secret, will reward you. And when you pray, do not keep on babbling like pagans, for they think they will be heard because of their many words. Do not be like them, for your Father knows what you need before you ask him. . . . For if you forgive others when they sin against you, your heavenly Father will also forgive you. But if you do not forgive others their sins, your Father will not forgive your sins."

—Matthew 6:5-8, 14

Sometimes people pray to other people: we lift our hands up in prayer so that others can see, or we lift our voices up primarily so that others can hear.

It's a problem of hypocrites and pontificators, actors and orators. Also of pastors and writers. In fact it's a problem of pray-ers in general.

By the grace of God, I have held my dream job for the last three years: minister for prayer in the Reformed Church in America. Why is this a dream job? Because I "love to pray standing in the synagogues and street corners."

Just last Sunday, I was praying on the street corners of downtown Holland, Michigan—standing at an intersection right across from my old junior high school. I was praying and I was loving it.

I love to pray with people not just on the streets, but in churches (the "synagogues" of our day). What a privilege to pray to the Resurrection and the Life while standing in front of bereaved people at a funeral! How strategic to pray on behalf of God's people through a portion of a Sunday morning service.

I love to stand and pray, and therein lies the problem. As soon as I start thinking about others looking at me, I become an actor—a *hupokrites*. I lose my focus. Worse yet, I forget my identity. Rather than seeing Jesus ahead on the path, I get distracted and diverted. Before I know it, I cannot see where Jesus is going and I cannot remember where I have been.

Worse even than what hypocritical prayer does to me is what it does to others. If what I do draws attention to me, then it necessarily draws attention

Word Alert

Hypocrite **comes from the Greek *hupokrites*, an actor, one who acts on stage. There's nothing wrong with the acting profession, but there's something terribly wrong if our lives and actions are for others to see rather than for service to God. So serious is the danger that Jesus rather humorously suggests that when doing good, we shouldn't "let our left hand know what the right hand is doing" (Matt. 6:3).**

away from God. I become an American Idol rather than a disciple of Jesus. Instead of leading people to God, I distance them.

Forgive me Lord, for the times I have prayed to be seen by others. Forgive me also for the times I have written to be heard for my many words.

I like polishing words. I am writing this daily reading because I think that a few well-chosen words might inspire people to pray. Yet I can lose my focus in words and phrases. Instead of praying in Jesus' name, I can start writing in Jonathan's name. So I need to return often to Paul's words: "My message and my preaching were not with wise and persuasive words, but with a demonstration of the Spirit's power" (1 Cor. 2:4).

I have noticed that my wife, Jeannette, who is *not* used to public speaking or professional writing, is more likely to ask the Holy Spirit's help before she does either. I, on the other hand, often depend more on my own skills than on the Holy Spirit's power.

There's a reason Jesus said, "Go into your room, close the door, and pray to your Father." Public prayer isn't wrong, but it can be dangerous. Let's just say that for every minute of public prayer before a congregation or before a meal, there should be more time in your room alone with God.

Lord, give me broken words to go with a broken heart! Let my polished pen be matched with a pure life.

Think It Over

1. How has the temptation of hypocrisy in prayer affected you?
2. How do you fight against it?

In Other Words

"We are made to want notice. One of the most characteristic remarks of the child is 'Watch me!' The child's verbal 'watch me' becomes the adult's more unspoken . . . 'notice me.' This drive to be noticed is not only the result of our sin, it is also a part of the image of God. We are made to notice and be noticed by God. . . ."

—Frederick Dale Bruner, *The Christbook*

Live It Out

End with a time of silent confession for the ways in which you have been hypocritical in your practice of prayer.

Feelings 5

"Why, my soul, are you downcast? Why so disturbed within me? Put your hope in God, for I will yet praise him, my Savior and my God."

—Psalm 42:5

We sometimes have the idea that our feelings and our faith go together like Frank Sinatra's horse and carriage. The fact is, they often don't. When we gather for worship, singing and lifting our hands and hearts in praise to God, we might be thinking about the argument we had last night. When we pray our minds often wander and our feelings can be flat. Does that mean our spiritual life is dead or dying? Do feelings tell us how things really are between us and God?

We live in a culture of spectacle, in which each rock concert, each television extravaganza, each political ad is engineered to manipulate our feelings. And churches aren't far behind. Just look at the beaming faces of the folks in the praise band as they lift the mikes to their mouths. How joyful they are, how ecstatic with praise! How close to God they must feel! And we're supposed to feel that way too.

Feelings are fickle. They're an important and real and even wonderful part of being human, but they aren't a very reliable measure of our relationship with God. Feelings don't tell the whole truth.

So how do we handle feelings in prayer?

First, realize that your feelings do not and cannot draw an accurate picture of your relationship with God. Anyone who has been married for some time understands this. There are times when a married couple feels very much "in love," but there are other times when they feel very little love. Sometimes they feel anger or resentment or boredom. Do those feelings define the relationship? No, it's their commitment that defines the love that holds them together, not their feelings at any given moment.

Our relationship with God—and prayer is near its core—depends on God's faithful, steady, covenant love, not on our feelings about God or ourselves or the world in general. Like a long marriage, our relationship with God may go through many phases and ignite many different feelings along the way. Or that relationship may suffer from a lack of feelings altogether in a kind of spiritual loneliness and desolation.

Many of the great spiritual pioneers have had this experience. One called it the "dark night of the soul." Recently the media reported that Mother Teresa suffered from this lack of spiritual feeling though most of her ministry. Does that mean her life was a sham? Hardly. It means her life was a monument to faith and courage.

Second, the secret of dealing with our feelings is to pray *through* them, not *with* them. If you feel a wonderfully deep attachment to your *Abba* in heaven one day, thank God for it, but don't expect you will feel that way tomorrow. Or just because you feel desolate and alone one day, don't give up on your prayers.

The psalmist asks, "Why should I feel downcast? Put your hope in God!" In other words, feelings don't really matter that much, God's love is what matters. Keep on praying, keep on trusting in spite of what you feel.

In an odd metaphor, C. S. Lewis once likened persistent prayer to digging ditches in a dry land. You keep on digging so that when the water comes, there's a ready channel for it. When we keep on praying through the spiritual drought, we'll be ready when the Spirit rains joy, strength, and peace on our dry souls.

"Put your hope in God. I will yet praise him, my Savior and my God."

Think It Over

1. How have negative feelings or a lack of feeling affected your prayer life?
2. What importance do you give to feelings in your spiritual life?

In Other Words

"To pray by feelings is to be at the mercy of glands and weather and digestion. And there is no mercy in any of them."

—Eugene Petersen, *Answering God*

Live It Out

As you pray today, think about how you're feeling spiritually. Offer it to God, put it into words, and then set it aside, knowing that it cannot govern how you pray or determine your relationship with God.

Session 4
The Problems of Prayer
Discussion Guide

Prayer may be one of the most discussed and least practiced priorities in the Christian life. Nobody thinks prayer is unimportant. Yet few Christians feel good about their practice of prayer. In this session we will face some of the problems people typically have with their understanding of prayer, as well as its practice.

This kind of an effort requires honesty. Saying anything negative about prayer is like saying something against your mother. And exposing our prayerlessness makes us feel spiritually naked. Yet if we don't honestly address our problems with prayer, we won't grow in our life as disciples.

So let's think deeply about this together. What is it that keeps us from praying more? Do we wonder whether God answers? Do we need more discipline in how regularly we ask? Does our view of God get in the way? How about the influence of others? Are we concerned about what others see or hear when we pray publicly? Perhaps we have a problem with the language of prayer. Why do we have to say it if God knows it?

Perhaps your problem with prayer hasn't been addressed in these daily readings. But you can share it with the group. Is it painful, practical, theological? Are you hung up on being a hypocrite, or tongue-tied, or just tired? Let the group know. Your prayer life is too important to let anything get in the way.

Word Alert

We often speak of *answers* to prayer. Most of the time we're referring not just to any answers but to specific answers—answers we can see, answers with measurable results. It's important to realize that God "answers" in many ways—some we can see by sight; others we can see only by faith.

Instead of saying "I *should* pray more but . . ." try saying "I *would* pray more if . . ." (for example, I would pray more if I knew God were listening, or if I could find the right words). Find the problem and pray it out.

For Starters

(15 minutes)

For a lighthearted beginning **share with the group your favorite answering machine message**. What do you like or not like about it? Imagine what kind of answering machine message you might like from God.

Then invite the members of the group to share one insight, surprise, or question they ran across from the devotional readings. Don't discuss it now, just mention it and what it meant to you.

Let's Focus

(2 minutes)

Read the introduction to this session and then have someone read this focus statement aloud:

To paraphrase G. K. Chesterton on the whole Christian life: Prayer has not been tried and found wanting. It has been found difficult and left untried. The practice of prayer is close to the heart of the Christian life, but it is not easy. Most Christians have problems understanding how prayer operates or lack the discipline to pray regularly. As we discuss the problems of prayer, the goal is to grow in the practice of prayer by facing and understanding its obstacles.

Word Search

(20 minutes)

Read aloud the following Scripture passages and briefly discuss at least some of the questions under each one (or formulate a better one of your own).

- Genesis 18:16-33
  Name some of the characteristics of Abraham's prayer for Sodom.

  How does this prayer address some of the "problems" discussed this week?
- Luke 22:41-43
  What does Jesus' prayer in the Garden of Gethsemane teach you about prayer?

  What is his message to the disciples and us about prayer?

  Jesus finally says, "Your will be done." Can this phrase also become a copout in the struggle of prayer?
- Luke 18:1-8
  What is the purpose of this parable, according to Jesus?

  How might you apply it to your life? Try to use specific examples.

Bring It Home

(20 minutes)

Choose one of these options:

Option 1

On a board, newsprint, or some other surface (preferably not the wall!) work together as a group to **come up with a short prayer that illustrates each of the problems of prayer discussed this week.** Or invite members of the group to pick a problem and write their own brief prayer that illustrates it. Then share the prayers with the group.

Option 2

Discuss *some* of these questions as time allows, or you may decide to take up a problem or question group members highlighted earlier from the devotional readings.

- What is the major obstacle to your life of prayer? Are there others that were not mentioned that you struggle with?
- Do you feel guilty about your prayer life? Is that a help or a hindrance to prayer?
- Do you wonder whether your prayers make any difference in the long run? Have you learned anything this week that encourages you in your struggles with prayer?
- What do you think might help you to become more disciplined in your prayer life?

Option 3

Distribute paper and pencils and **invite group members to illustrate where they are in their prayer life.** It may be a problem, a feeling, a need—anything that gets at their own issues with prayer. Try to use diagrams or illustrations instead of words to get at these issues.

Pray It Through

(10 minutes)

Take time to suggest items to pray about together. These may be items of praise, thanksgiving, confession, or request—and especially issues raised by this session.

Or, as you have come to understand each other's problems and difficulties with prayer, invite each member to pray about the specific struggles of the person to the right as you move around the circle.

Live It Out

(5-15 minutes each day during the coming week)

Many spiritual teachers recommend a prayer plan, or "rule of prayer." Think, pray, and perhaps discuss with a trusted friend who knows you well what your own discipline of prayer might look like. You might like to write it down and begin practicing it this week. Try to include when and how you might pray and list some of the tools you might wish to use in prayer.

Web Alert

Be sure to check the participants' section for this session on www.GrowDisciples.org for all kinds of interesting links and suggestions for readings and activities that will deepen your understanding and experience of prayer.

Session 5

Ways of Praying

Alone 1

"Jesus, full of the Holy Spirit, left the Jordan and was led by the Spirit into the wilderness, where for forty days he was tempted by the devil."

—Luke 4:1-2b

There are two "forces" trying to get Jesus alone: the Holy Spirit and the devil.

That's true for us too. The Holy Spirit wants us alone to talk to us. The devil wants us alone to taunt us. The Spirit directs; the devil destroys. The Spirit empowers; the devil implodes. The devil's schemes are to divide and devour—get one sheep away from the flock and tear it to pieces. The Spirit seeks to unite and feed. Satan and Spirit, the devil and the divine: both have an interest in us when we are alone.

Alone in the desert with the Spirit, Jesus hears the familiar words of the Torah: "People do not live on bread alone"; "Worship the Lord your God and serve him only"; "Do not put the Lord your God to the test." When Jesus is with other people, his attention is divided—he is listening to them. By going to a solitary place, Jesus can listen solely to the Father's voice.

Jesus grew up studying the Torah—the first five books of the Bible, from which these words come.

Could Jesus have heard from the Father without going into the desert? Luke seems to say no. Jesus has to go into the desert alone and fast *in order to* hear from God. This is a necessary solitude. Jesus *needs* alone time with Father and Spirit.

Word Alert

***Fasting* is a spiritual discipline that involves going without food for a period of time for spiritual purposes—to pay special attention to what God may be saying to us. It's different from dieting, which is done in order to lose weight.**

Jesus doesn't find more of the Spirit in the wilderness. In fact, throughout his whole life, from the time he was "conceived by the Holy Spirit" and anointed with the Spirit in his baptism (Luke 3:22), there was never a time when he was without the Spirit. Jesus is already "full of the Holy Spirit" before going off to be alone (Luke 4:1).

The Spirit leads Jesus to a solitary place in order to empower him for ministry. Jesus hears and experiences things during his time alone in prayer that he would not otherwise experience. That's why Jesus made a habit of getting away to pray (Luke 5:15-16; Mark 1:35).

We need to visit solitary places too. In the midst of our crowded cities, busy lives, and the constant voices of the media, we need to talk and listen to God directly and personally.

There are times when the Spirit may lead us "to a solitary place." But those times when we're alone may also be occasions for the devil to try to get at us. So what happens when we get to our secret places? What are the secrets of our secret places? These are important prayer questions.

Let's look at a couple of scenarios. A businessman checks into the hotel where he is staying for two nights. A Gideons' Bible lies in the drawer. A TV with pay-per-view porn rests on the dresser. Will he be driven by a demon or led by the Spirit? What will happen in this solitary place? Will he pray, "Lead us not into temptation, but deliver us from evil"? Or will he pander to the temptation? What would we do?

Or consider a mother with a busy schedule. At the end of a long day at work, she finally finds a few moments alone to consider her "empty nest." She thinks of her two children—now well into their twenties. She knows they do not attend church. She has doubts about the strength of their faith and about their lifestyles. She is prompted to pray for them, but she also hears a wicked whisper: "You have failed as a mother; all you have sacrificed for them is lost. . . ." What does she do? To whom will she listen in this solitary place? What would we do?

Here's the point. Solitude in itself is neither good nor bad. It all depends on what we do with it. In all likelihood, if we leave our time alone open—that is, unplanned and undirected toward God—it will become an opportunity for the devil.

If we don't plan and pray in ways that help us hear from God in our times alone, we are liable to hear from someone else. Why not plan today some time of prayer alone with God? Of all the things we do when we are alone, could anything be better?

Think It Over

1. Do you specifically plan some time each day to be alone with God? What might happen if you did?
2. What happens in those alone times when God is not invited?

In Other Words

"The careful balance between silence and words, withdrawal and involvement, distance and closeness, solitude and community forms the basis for the Christian life and should be the subject of our most personal attention."

—Henri J. M. Nouwen, *Out of Solitude*

Live It Out

As you go through the day, notice the times you are alone (in the car, at the office, at home). What happens in those times? What fills the "void"? Commit to using some of those times to draw closer to God by listening to what he may have to say to you. For example, if you always listen to the radio while you're driving, you may want to turn it off once in a while and lift up your heart to God.

Together 2

"Again, I tell you that if two of you on earth agree about anything you ask for, it will be done for you by my Father in heaven. For where two or three come together in my name, there am I with them."

—Matthew 18:19-20

I can remember sitting in a hard wooden church pew at Trinity Reformed Church in Holland, Michigan. I spent a lot of time "browsing the bulletin." Our church had this strange-looking image on every bulletin. It was the old logo insignia of the Reformed Church in America—the coat of arms of William of Orange. You don't see it many places anymore. Once I found the coat of arms, I would whisper to my mom to hand me a pencil. And then I would treat that diagram like a coloring book.

In my coloring, though, I missed the Dutch words that go with the insignia: *Eendracht maakt macht,* which means, "In unity there is strength." (I sometimes wonder what strengths the Reformed Church in American and the Christian Reformed Church might have displayed had we remained united instead of separating 150 years ago!)

The founders of the Reformed Church may not have had Jesus' words in mind when they chose that motto, but it certainly fits with Jesus' promise that our prayers have a special strength when we pray with others: "If two of you . . . agree about anything . . . it will be done for you. . . ." What a broad and generous promise!

Solitary prayer, as we've learned, is essential to our spiritual health. And praying together is essential to our spiritual power. We see that in the book of Acts. The disciples gathered daily for prayer at the Lord's command from his ascension to the astounding gift of the Holy Spirit at Pentecost. Afterward they continued to gather daily for prayer, as the Lord added to their numbers daily (Acts 2:42-47).

Jeremiah Calvin Lanphier was hired as a lay missionary in connection with the North Dutch Reformed Church in New York, just a few blocks from where the World Trade Center once stood. He felt it would be profitable to challenge men to meet regularly at noon for a time of prayer together. So he established a time of prayer on Wednesdays from noon to one o' clock in the consistory building on Fulton Street.

The first meeting of what came to be known as the Fulton Street Prayer Revival took place on September 23, 1857. The first person to join Lanphier was a half-hour late; several others came even later. Five denominations were represented. The following week, twenty attended. The third week, there were forty. By the fourth week, they decided to hold a meeting every workday. The prayer revival grew to include Christians from a variety of denominations;

within months, meetings were being held throughout the city. The movement soon spread to other cities from coast to coast.

This Fulton Street prayer meeting continued until 1961. No one can calculate what these prayers accomplished for over a century, but I do not doubt that hundreds, even thousands of lives were changed because of it, and the church grew and deepened in faith.

There is a special power in agreeing together in prayer. One group with whom I pray regularly has the practice of verbally "agreeing" in prayer—if one person prays for something, others in the group will say yes, or yes, Lord, or just amen. I always sense the power of this agreement, and it helps me pray with greater faith.

"I am with them." Jesus not only promises power but presence in a group—even "two or three"—that gathers in his name. The famous Los Angeles Bible teacher Dr. Henrietta Mears once said that Jesus made this promise to two or three because he knew that was about as many as could be expected at the typical prayer meeting!

Of course it's not the numbers that count. It's the dedication and the direction of the group. Even two or three disciples dedicated to serving Jesus have his presence and the promise of his power.

Perhaps the most important meeting you can attend outside of worship is a prayer meeting, no matter how small. You won't find them in too many churches today. But wherever you do find them, you can be sure that Jesus is there and his power is being unleashed.

Think It Over

1. What experiences have you had of corporate prayer? What was good about it? What was difficult or problematic?
2. What do you think keeps us from praying together more regularly?

In Other Words

"The smallest group of Christians—even a couple—enjoys the largest promise of God—Jesus. This should encourage Christian couples [and small groups]—together in prayer they constitute a veritable temple and so they can expect miracles with their children, their congregations, and with the Christian mission in the world."

—Frederick Dale Bruner, *The Churchbook*

Live It Out

Get together with at least one other person in prayer today. Agree with them in prayer on something that's on your hearts.

Liturgy 3

"They devoted themselves to the apostles' teaching and to fellowship, to the breaking of bread and to prayer. . . . Every day they continued to meet together in the temple courts. . . . One day Peter and John were going up to the temple at the time of prayer—at three in the afternoon."

—Acts 2:42, 46; 3:1

I once attended a very "liturgical" church. The sermon was unorganized and unbiblical. What saved that congregation from wasting its time was the liturgy. That sturdy liturgy, right from a prayer book, brought us through all the movements of prayer: praise, confession, Scripture, creed, and petition.

Liturgy is not a particularly popular word for most Reformed folks. Sometimes we equate liturgy with lethargy. Our tradition has prized spontaneous, extemporaneous prayer over written prayer. The more spontaneous the more "spiritual"; the more liturgical the less authentic. But that's a false dichotomy. Spontaneous prayers can be dead on the lips, while written prayers can sing our heart's deepest longing. It's the direction of our hearts that counts.

Throughout the centuries faithful Christians have prayed "by the book"—that is, they have used the words and prayers of others to prime the pump of their own devotional life. Biblical scholars can reconstruct the daily and weekly worship of the Jewish temple and synagogue, and it is quite certain that early Christians modeled their own prayer on what they experienced there. It was liturgical prayer.

Some people seem to think that since prayer is simply talking to God, we should just start talking. But I wonder what gives us the idea that prayer is easy, or that the words of prayer should easily pour from our minds and lips. It's my experience that after a few days or weeks of listening to my own silent thoughts or spoken yammering, I get sick of the sound of my own inner voice. My impromptu words of praise seem shallow and banal; my petitions strike me as selfish and narrow.

Some may find using others' written prayers boring. But many others find them useful and even inspiring ways to prime the pump of their own prayer life. Perhaps it helps to think of each written prayer, each liturgy, as somebody's love letter to God. It may not be everyone's love letter, but somewhere along the line, someone put pen to paper out of devotion to God. And someone else will want to experience it.

It's a bit like buying and sending cards to express our feelings on birthdays, holidays, and anniversaries. I suppose it would be more authentic if each of us sent hand-made cards with our own well-crafted greetings. But Hallmark doesn't seem to be going out of business any time soon.

Personally, I prefer lots of white space on my greeting cards. I like cards that "say it simple" and give me room to add my own two cents. Others prefer to have someone else "say it" for them. They take the time to pick out just the right card, one that expresses on paper what is in their heart.

Paul says, "Let the message of Christ dwell among you richly as you teach and admonish one another with all wisdom through psalms, hymns and songs from the Spirit" (Col. 3:16). If a psalm says it best, pray a psalm. If an old hymn expresses what you feel deeply, sing the words as your prayer.

The sixty-member church I serve offers a class called "The Gospel in Hymns." We study the great hymns of the faith from a hymnal, and we sing them with the accompaniment of an iPod. We are using liturgical forms to aid our prayer.

And don't overlook prayer books like the *Book of Common Prayer.* This book and others are used by millions to anchor their daily prayer with fine, sturdy prayers lovingly penned by faithful Christians over the years. And these prayers are structured into a liturgy that includes praise, Psalms, Scriptures, confession, and room for silent prayers. They're a gift that can help each of us as we look for ways to nurture a vigorous prayer life.

Remember that you're not alone in your commitment to pray. You have the treasury of the centuries-old prayers of the church at your disposal.

Web Alert

If you're interested in experimenting with a prayer book, many are available to check out free in a web-based format. See www.GrowDisciples.org for this session.

Think It Over

1. Have you used some form of written prayers for your personal devotions?
2. How do you feel about the contrast between spontaneous and more liturgical or written prayer?

In Other Words

"We all need structure in our lives, and our prayers can benefit too. There's an ironic freedom that comes from not having to concentrate on what I'm going to say in prayer. It's right there in the book! That feels good in the fog of early morning or the tiredness of evening."

—Leonard Vander Zee, "Praying by the Book," *The Banner* (August 2001)

Live It Out

Consider using this evening prayer as you go to bed each night this week:

Keep watch, dear Lord, with those who work or watch or weep this night, and give your angels charge over those who sleep. Tend the sick, Lord Christ; give rest to the weary, bless the dying, soothe the suffering, pity the afflicted, shield the joyous; and all for your love's sake. Amen.

Spontaneity 4

"Do not be anxious about anything, but in every situation, by prayer and petition, with thanksgiving, present your requests to God."

—Philippians 4:6

Written, liturgical prayer can be loving prayer. It can also be dead and legalistic. Liturgy, if we are not careful, can lead to observing a "form of godliness but denying its power" (2 Tim. 3:5). Rigidity rather than relationship can become our overriding value.

The care we take with written prayers can reflect how we value prayer. It can also, however, simply mean we value control. We can plan the Spirit right out of our prayers and put our own desires there instead.

Think of it this way. If planned, written, liturgical prayer is the skeleton of our prayer life, spontaneous, continuous eruptions of prayer is its flesh and blood.

Be ready to pray "continually," Paul writes (1 Thess. 5:17). People have tried to figure out what that means for a long time. I think it simply means that we go through our days in a constant attitude of prayer. We practice faith rather than anxiety, thankfulness rather than boredom. In the words of a devotional classic on prayer, we "practice the presence of God."

We catch something of what this is like in Paul's letters. He begins his letter to the Colossians by saying, "We always thank God . . . when we pray for you." A few verses later he continues, "We continually ask God to fill you with the knowledge of his will . . . so that you may live a life worthy of the Lord . . . bearing fruit in every good work, growing in the knowledge of God" (Col. 1:3-10). It's hard to tell where the letter ends and the prayer begins. That's the way it is with spontaneous, continuous prayer.

It means praying for our neighbors as we ride down the street on the way to work. It means asking God for patience and understanding when we feel our anger rise at a coworker's ineptitude. It means thanking God for the countless gifts of grace we encounter through the day. It means admitting our sin when our thoughts go to revenge or lust.

Pray anywhere and pray anytime. Pray when you get up in the morning. I know someone, for instance, whose first waking moment is a kneeling moment, right beside the bed. Wash your sins away with soap, making your shower a prayer of confession. Put on your clothes the way Paul recommends we put on spiritual armor in Ephesians 6. Walk out the door, remembering the doorposts Deuteronomy 6 invites us to mark with Scripture. Give thanks for living water as you drink. Praying for daily bread when you eat. Walk "in the Spirit." Breathe the breath of God. Declare God's kindness in the morning and his faithfulness throughout the night.

Turn all your experiences, all your daily activities, even all your thoughts into prayer. That's living moment by moment before the face of God. That's spontaneous, constant prayer.

Some people may find it frightening to think of prayer that way—but why? It's only frightening if we don't really believe that our lives are redeemed and our sins are forgiven in the blood of Christ. It's only frightening if we feel we need to hold some hidden corner of our lives back from God.

Spontaneity isn't the enemy of liturgy in prayer. They're more like partners. Spontaneity can be the flesh of everyday life wrapping around a sturdy skeleton of liturgy and written prayer.

Think It Over

1. Do you practice spontaneous prayer through the day? Why or why not?
2. How might a more constant practice of prayer change your life?

In Other Words

"Prayer is a radical conversion of all our mental processes, because in prayer we move away from ourselves—our worries, preoccupations, and self-gratifications—and direct all that we recognize as ours to God in the simple trust that through his love all will be made new."

—Henri J. M. Nouwen, *Clowning in Rome*

Live It Out

Try to practice spontaneous and constant prayer today. Be gentle with yourself when you discover that hours have gone by with barely a thought or word directed toward God. But when it works, notice what it does to you.

Variety 5

"And pray in the Spirit on all occasions with all kinds of prayers and requests. With this in mind, be alert and always keep on praying for all the Lord's people."

—Ephesians 6:18

"And whatever you do, whether in word or deed, do it all in the name of the Lord Jesus, giving thanks to God the Father through him."

—Colossians 3:17

There's a difference between creation and duplication, between copying and designing. God creates; he deals only in original art. We, on the other hand, sometimes treat our prayers like photocopies. We come up with a system, an "original," and then we put the original in a machine and make multiple copies.

Our prayers need not be photocopies of some original we've developed or been taught over the years. Variety in God's creation begs for variety in our conversation with God.

The danger of this or any study of prayer for disciples is that it becomes prescriptive rather than evocative. So keep in mind that this is a start, not a summary. It's a beginning, not an ending.

The ideas in this book are suggestions, not straightjackets for how to approach God.

I don't want you to wear my own prayer habits like an awkward-fitting piece of clothing. And I certainly don't want you to feel you have to wear them every time you want to come to God.

Word Alert

***Habit* is one of those multiple-use words that lends itself to wordplay. It's a behavior pattern that we fall into almost without thinking. And it's an old word for the distinctive clothes of monks and nuns in religious orders.**

Perhaps you've noticed one thing over the course of these daily readings: There is a variety of gifts, and there are all kinds of prayers.

Each of us is unique, and each of us will find a way of praying that fits our personality and temperament. It's unlikely, for instance, that an introvert's prayer life will thrive best in the many voices of a prayer meeting. An extrovert, on the other hand, might find it difficult to spend hours in solitude. It's perfectly natural to carve out a style of prayer that fits who we are.

One person may pray best with a prayer list, checking items off with thanksgiving as prayers are answered or problems solved. Another person prays best while dancing slowly through her house, or while listening to music with an iPod. Still another prays on his daily jog. One couple begins the day by visiting one of many websites that offer daily prayer liturgies.

It's good for us to stretch our experience of prayer too. If we always avoid solitude, we may well miss coming face to face with ourselves before God. If we avoid prayer groups, we might never learn the comfort and strength of "agreeing" in prayer.

Pray without words and pray with words. Let there be silence in your prayer closet, or let there be rock and roll music in your garage.

Let there be *lectio divina*, a worshipful, quiet, prayerful reading of the Scriptures. Why not? What a wonderful way to let the Scriptures lead directly into the prayer of the heart!

Let there be "breath prayers," short phrases that express our deepest desires that we offer to God hundreds of time throughout the day. Pray alone or pray together with others. Pray from a book or pray by heart.

Pray on all occasions. The early church prays at the colonnade and in the Temple. They pray in the upper room and pray beside the river. They pray when they eat and they pray when they don't eat. There is prayer and fasting and there is prayer and feasting.

Pray with all kinds of prayer. At a denominational gathering, I was introduced to *centering prayer*. I had concerns about whether it was biblical. I had questions about how practical it was. But I gave it a try and in the trying found fresh peace and purpose in this prayer of stillness and listening.

There are so many different ways people pray in the Bible. We have talked about lots of them during our time together with these daily readings. There are also so many different ways Christians have prayed down through history. Study the great Christian masters of prayer through the ages.

Web Alert

Make a special point of checking the web extras at www.GrowDisciples.org for this session. There are lots of links where you can learn more about the different kinds of prayer mentioned here, as well as others.

Prayer isn't just talking with God; it's the myriad ways in which we live in relationship with God. Like any relationship it may take many forms and it may change through the years.

So whatever you do, "keep on praying" (Eph. 6:18). "Always pray and do not give up" (Luke 18:1).

Think It Over

List some of the ways you pray. If you can only think of one or two, try to identify others ways that may be particularly well-suited to your personality.

In Other Words

"God's invitation [to prayer] . . . is not casual; it is an invitation from his very heart to the depths of our being. It warrants serious consideration because it is an invitation to a journey, a quest really. . . . Unlike a trip designed to get us somewhere as efficiently as possible, a quest requires us to leave familiar dwelling places for strange lands we cannot yet envision, without knowing when we will return."

—Ruth Haley Barton, *Invitation to Solitude and Silence*

Live It Out

If there is one among the variety of ways of praying that struck you as interesting or worth exploring, take some time to read about it and practice it today.

Session 5
Ways of Praying
Discussion Guide

Most people, when asked to define prayer, would answer something like this: Prayer is talking with God. That's true—but it's also much more. It encompasses our whole relationship with God. And it's one of the primary means of building that relationship.

Imagine a married couple. Talking to each other is certainly a primary way of communication and relationship-building. But it's not the only way. Think of some of the other ways they communicate: through look and touch, for instance. Shared experiences and shared silences. The many syllables of body language.

Not surprisingly, many of us are used to one or perhaps two ways of praying—it's what we were taught. But we find an astounding variety of ways of praying in the Bible itself, as well as in the Christian tradition through the ages. This week we will explore some of that variety in hopes that it will whet your appetite for further exploration.

Word Alert

***Body language* is the way we express our thoughts and feelings, often involuntarily. It doesn't take much practice to read the gestures, movements, and tics by which our body "speaks." During an interview with a young married couple, the wife was complaining about some of her husband's bad habits. The husband smiled and seemed to accept what she was saying, except that he was constantly flicking lint and dust off his trousers with his forefinger as each habit was mentioned.**

For Starters

(10 minutes)

Share one insight, surprise, or question you encountered in the daily readings this week. Don't discuss it now, just mention it and what it meant to you.

Let's Focus

(2 minutes)

Read the introduction to this session and then have someone read this focus statement aloud:

Prayer is turning our hearts to God. It's the heartbeat of our relationship with God. Our prayer life is diminished when that relationship takes only one or two forms. It will grow as we learn more about our personal preferences in prayer and explore the wealth of resources provided throughout the whole Christian tradition.

Word Search

(20 minutes)

Read aloud the following Scripture passages and briefly discuss some of the questions under each one (or formulate better questions of your own).

- Mark 1:34-36
  Notice that this comes at the end of a description of one very busy day in Jesus' life. What led Jesus to this "solitary place"?

  Do you have a solitary place? What are its joys and difficulties?

- Acts 4:23-31
  What are some of the characteristics of this "prayer meeting?"

  How did the people address God, and what effect do you think it had?

  How did they use Scripture in their prayer? What was the result?

- Psalm 131
  What picture of prayer does this evoke?

  What would this kind of prayer look like in your life?

Bring It Home

(20 minutes)

Choose one of the following options:

Option 1

Go around the group and have each person describe one or two key aspects of his or her God-given personality. Then have the group **suggest ways of praying that might especially suit that person's traits.**

Option 2

Discuss *some* of the following questions as time allows. Alternatively, you may decide to take up a problem or question group members highlighted earlier from the devotional readings.

- Would you say that you are "stuck" with one or two ways of praying? How did that happen? What are you going to do about it?
- Of the various ways of praying described in the devotional readings this week, which appealed to you the most? The least? Why?
- Prayer is not just talking to God, it's also listening to him. How might that happen? How might you hear God's voice?

Option 3

Think of someone you particularly admire as a man or woman of prayer. Give a brief description of that person's life of prayer. Does it point to any of the variety of ways of praying we've been discussing this week? Does it suggest new ways of praying?

Pray It Through

(10 minutes)

Since this is the last group session on prayer, take special care to plan your prayer time. Here are a few options to consider:

- Let each person take a turn sitting in the center while the other group members gather around. As group members lay a hand on the shoulder or back of the person, invite them to pray that the Spirit will strengthen and nourish this person's life of prayer and overcome any obstacles or problems.
- Pray as usual for each other in the ways you have practiced as a group. Then end the prayer by reading together Paul's prayer in Ephesians 3:14-21, taking care to change the "you" and "your" to "us" and "our." (It may be helpful to make a photocopy of the prayer with the changes made ahead of time.)
- Invite someone beforehand to construct a printed and photocopied "liturgical prayer" to be spoken together or responsively. You may wish to use the resources provided in the many online prayer sites, such as www.oremus.org.

Live It Out

(5-15 minutes each day during the coming week)

Prayer is not easy. It's a long quest, an arduous journey, and it's easy to become discouraged. Throughout the centuries pioneers of prayer have advised Christians to find a prayer guide, friend, or partner. Such a person has been called a variety of terms: "spiritual director," soul friend," "prayer partner." By whatever name, this is simply a person who will sit with you, support you, and encourage you in the adventure of building a relationship with God through prayer. Take the time this week as the Spirit leads to pray, think, and act toward this kind of partnership.

Web Alert

Be sure to check the participants' section for this session on www.GrowDisciples.org for all kinds of interesting links and suggestions for readings and activities that will deepen your understanding and experience of prayer.